WINNING is not a
STRATEGY

A Game-Changing Approach
to Driving Attendance

by ZAC LOGSDON

BLACK LAKE
PUBLISHING COMPANY

Black Lake Publishing, LLC
102 West Eufaula, Suite 200
Norman, OK 73069

First edition, October 2018
ISBN: 9781644679852

Table of Contents

PREGAME

Sports marketing is fascinating. Over the past two decades I've had a front row seat and backstage pass to some of the best and worst efforts in the business. Nearly 20 years ago I began my career in athletics, working for the University of Oklahoma before starting a strategic marketing company in 2004 called Old Hat. In that time, I have worked with more than 150 sports organizations in all leagues and on all levels to help with their marketing efforts. Working in athletics from both inside and outside athletics organizations has given me a unique perspective on what the industry does well and where it falls short.

In the fall of 2016, I set out to write a sports marketing book. My goal was to outline my observations and offer advice on how the athletics industry should adjust its approach and become more effective at putting fans in the stands.

I had planned to include an introductory chapter on the power of sports because the amazing memories I've made through athletics are what fuel my passion for this line of work. I thought it would be helpful to include stories from athletics administrators about times when they witnessed just how truly impactful sports can be. As I interviewed administrators from programs of all sizes nationwide, I was awed by what I heard. The more people I interviewed, the more I realized those stories deserved to stand on their own. That book, *If Not for Athletics*, was published in June 2017 and has been very well received both inside and outside the athletics industry.

So what about all those opinions I wanted to share about how the industry should adapt to an ever-changing market? My editor finally convinced me to save it for a second book, which made *If Not for Athletics* a far better book than it would have been otherwise and led me to develop the book you're reading now. If anything, *If Not for Athletics* reinforced my conviction that sports marketers need to change their way of thinking. Attendance at sporting events is declining, and people can't fully experience the transformative power of sports by watching a game at home on the couch. I wanted to do something to help the industry ensure these types of experiences aren't lost on the next generation.

Welcome to *Winning is Not a Strategy*, a book that has been 20 years in the making. While much of this is my opinion, I believe you will find that most of those opinions are backed by data and the science of human behavior. The sole purpose of this book is to give athletics professionals new ideas and tools to re-engage existing fans and appeal to new fans. I hope that anyone reading it can take at least one valuable bit of information from it and implement positive change within their athletics organization.

WINNING IS
NOT A STRATEGY

I began my first job in athletics in February 2001 as a graphic designer for the University of Oklahoma Athletics Department. I couldn't have been there more than a month before I heard it for the first time:

If we'd just start winning, attendance would take care of itself.

If I had a dollar for every time I've heard that statement or one like it since then, I'd be a rich man. Ok, maybe not rich - but I'd at least have a couple hundred bucks. While the exact statement can take many forms (*Fans don't want to come watch us lose* or *We wouldn't have attendance problems if the team didn't suck)*, the predominant philosophy is the same: fans attend sporting events to watch their team win. The assumption is that when the chances of winning decrease, so does attendance. Seems logical, right? It's hard to disagree with an idea that makes so much sense.

That concept is *so* difficult to disagree with, in fact, that virtually no one in the athletics industry disagrees with it. In the spring of 2016, Old Hat conducted a nationwide survey of athletics administrators to gain insight into a number of topics. When asked what they felt was the primary factor that determined whether or not fans would attend the game, the #1 response by an overwhelming margin was: *Whether or not the team is winning.* Imagine that for a moment. We work in an industry that charges us with getting fans to attend events yet we have zero control over the one thing we feel affects that decision more than anything else.

I have good news, though. The data doesn't support the idea that winning affects attendance nearly as much as we think it does. Winning helps, of course. No one would argue that it's just as easy to market a bad product as it is to market a good one. What I am arguing is that there are plenty of things that indicate one can effectively put fans in our stadiums and arenas regardless of how good the quality of play is. Moreover, there are even a larger number of examples of times when winning isn't solving the problem.

Attendance is Dropping

CBS Sports published an article in February 2018 with the headline: *College football heads in wrong direction with largest attendance drop in 34 years.*

Here are some of the statistics cited in the article:

- Attendance was down an average of 1,409 fans per game from 2016 to 2017 among the 129 Football Bowl Subdivision (FBS) teams.
- The 2017 FBS average attendance of 42,203 fans per game was the lowest since 1997. This drop in attendance was the second sharpest decline since attendance started being tracked in 1948.
- FBS attendance has dropped more than 10 percent over the past nine years.
- Student attendance has decreased 7 percent since 2009.

If you're reading this book, chances are that none of this comes as a surprise to you. You've probably either read that article or one of the plethora of other articles that have come out in recent years about attendance declines in both collegiate and professional athletics, in every league on every level. All of the data shows that each year, fewer and fewer people are attending sporting events. Yet the prevailing attitude toward solving this problem continues to be: *Win games and attendance will increase.*

Winning Isn't Everything

It's very difficult to determine just how much overall

Dodd, Dennis. "College football heads in wrong direction with largest attendance drop in 34 years." *CBSSports.com*, CBS Broadcasting Inc., 13 February 2018, https://www. cbssports.com/college-football/news/college-football-heads-in-wrong-direction-with-largest-attendance-drop-in-34-years/

attendance is affected by winning or any other single factor. Sometimes a team will have a great season and attendance will increase either immediately or in the following year. Other times attendance will spike due to a new coach or adjustments in pricing. Or you might have a program that experiences a decrease in attendance in any given year for no apparent reason, even when they've had a winning season the year prior.

Obviously winning has at least some effect on attendance and I'm not here to argue otherwise. However, evidence shows that a team's record has much less of an effect on putting fans in stands than we'd like to believe.

Let's take a look at this on a conference level.

Of the Power 5 conferences, the SEC is widely considered to have the best football programs across the board. Of the 20 national championship games played since the BCS/ CFP era, 11 have been won by SEC teams. The next closest is the ACC with three national championship game wins. Additionally, over the past five years the SEC has played in and won more bowl games than any other conference. The gap in total bowls and wins between the SEC and other Power 5 conferences isn't drastic, but the fact remains that the SEC just wins more than other conferences. Based on the idea that winning drives attendance, it would stand to reason that the SEC would have either an increase in attendance, no drop in attendance or (as a worst case scenario) the lowest drop in attendance when compared to other conferences.

But that's not the case. From 2016 to 2017, the SEC reported the *largest* drop in average attendance by nearly double any other conference. The only conference to report an increase in average attendance was the Big Ten, which is only one win ahead of last place in conference bowl wins in the past five years among its Power 5 peers.

The winningest conference in college football reported the largest drop in attendance while the conference that barely kept itself out of last place was the only one that reported an increase in attendance.

Interesting.

Need more evidence that winning isn't the magic wand we may think it is? Good. I have some.

Of the top 20 FBS teams ranked by attendance (the top 20 teams with the highest attendance), 13 actually had a decrease in attendance from 2016 to 2017. That's notable in and of itself because even the most well-attended programs are seeing decreases. But what's more interesting is that 6 of those 13 teams had actually improved their win-loss records from 2016 to 2017. They have a history of great attendance *and* were winning yet the increase in wins didn't equal an increase in attendance for them. And they're not alone.

In 2014, the number of teams that saw a decrease in attendance despite having a better record from the previous year was 28. That number continues to increase. A whopping

40 FBS college football programs experienced decreases in attendance in 2017 despite having better records than the year before. On the flip side, 20 programs actually had worse win-loss records in 2017 and *increased* attendance.

We're headed in the wrong direction and winning isn't solving the problem.

Case in Point: MLS

If the rule is that attendance increases with winning games and decreases with losing them, Major League Soccer (MLS) isn't playing by the rules at all. Looking at attendance versus win-loss record over the course of three seasons (2015-2017), the teams in the MLS seem to defy all logic when it comes to the theory that winning affects attendance.

There are 23 teams in the MLS. We'll be looking at data for 20 of those teams, because three (Los Angeles FC, Atlanta United FC and Minnesota United FC) are new enough to lack win-loss and attendance numbers for the full timeframe we're considering.

It's surprising to note that only one-fifth of the teams in the MLS follow the "rule" that attendance increases as a team achieves greater on-field success. Four out of 20 teams! That means eighty percent of the teams in the MLS operate outside of the assumed norm of how performance impacts attendance.

Measuring Success in Soccer

Soccer measures success a little differently than other sports. Rankings are determined based on a point system rather than strictly on wins and losses. A win earns a team 3 points, a loss earns 0 points and a draw or tie earns them 1 point.

Most MLS teams accumulate a point total somewhere in the forties or fifties. Only two teams achieved point totals over 60 during this study: in 2017, Sporting KC earned 67 points and Toronto FC earned 65. At the low end, a couple of teams only reached 32 points in 2017 and the Chicago Fire held the lowest point total of 31 in 2016. We can assume that anything above 50 would be considered a pretty successful season.

For the purposes of this argument, I am going by overall points and how that affects attendance (or doesn't).

Looking at the data, we can lump each team into one of three categories: rule followers, consistently inconsistent and rule breakers.

Rule Followers

Pretty self-explanatory here: for these teams, attendance and winning appear to go hand in hand. The Chicago Fire had 50 points in 2015 and an average attendance of about 16,000 fans. In 2016, their points dipped to 31 and they lost an average of about 400 fans per game. Then in 2017, their success spiked to 55 points and attendance increased by 1500 fans per game. Other teams that followed this trend were the Colorado Rapids, LA Galaxy and Toronto FC.

Consistently Inconsistent

This is the second largest group with six of the 20 teams falling into this category. For these teams, fan attendance behavior did not seem to correlate consistently with each team's on-field success or failure. For instance, the Seattle Sounders had a fairly significant drop in attendance from 2015 to 2016, despite having pretty much the same on-field success in both years. In 2017 they had their most successful season in terms of points and while attendance improved, it failed to reach 2015 levels. Sporting KC had virtually no change in attendance over the 3-year period despite highly inconsistent performance from season to season (although that may be because their attendance is consistently at maximum capacity). These and other teams in this category simply don't prove the theory correct or incorrect. But they do seem to show that increases and decreases in attendance don't seem to be too directly tied to on-field success.

Rule Breakers

This is my favorite category as they seem to defy common logic with regard to attendance. Not only is this the largest category, some of the data is mind-boggling. Every team in this category goes against the grain of the "rule." DC United has increased fan attendance nearly 10% every year despite having fewer and fewer points in each. FC Dallas had two highly successful seasons in 2015 and 2016 with the exact same number of points (60) in each, but saw a huge drop in attendance from one year to the next. Then in 2017, they had a significant drop in points (46) but a spike in attendance (back up by more than 1,000 fans per game). However, the best examples are teams like Real Salt Lake, which achieved consistently greater success each season (41, 46 and 51 points) but experienced a gradual decline in average attendance each year, and New York City FC, which also consistently improved its performance (37, 54 and 57 points) and had huge drops in average attendance each year.

I could go down the list and point out the contradictory data from more teams throughout the MLS or I could cite the hundreds of examples of teams that have had lackluster on-field performance but have enjoyed great attendance. I could talk about how the Green Bay Packers have sold out every game since 1960, even when their on-field performance wasn't great. I could talk about the Hamilton Tiger Cats or the Chicago Cubs and how their season ticket renewal rate and attendance defied all logic in years when the team was hardly winning at all. I could bring up MiLB's Richmond Flying Squirrels and how they lead the league in attendance every year despite finishing near the bottom of the rankings.

I could do that, but someone on the other side of the argument could then point out the hundreds of times a team started to win and fans started flooding to the games.

And one could definitely argue that there are many factors that could skew *all* of this data and that correlation doesn't necessarily imply causation. But the fact remains that when you compare all the available data, the connection between winning/losing and attendance is shaky at best.

The "rule" that states that winning teams generally see increases in attendance is undeniable. But the exciting part is that the preceding examples show that it's also undeniable that there are exceptions to the rule. What we have to do is find ways to make ourselves the exception and that's what this book intends to help you do.

Now, do most fans want to show up to watch terrible teams play? No. Are sporting events more fun if your favorite team plays well and is competitive? Of course. But our job as marketers is to create strategies that will drive fans to attend our events and have such an amazing time, they'll keep coming back. And *winning* is not a strategy.

Todd Albright
Director, Marketing & Fan Experience
Seattle Sounders

I think the unique thing about MLS, or soccer in general, is that it's built around the culture. Fans are a part of more than just a game and attend for more than just what's happening on the field. If you look at our supporter groups, for example, they chant, they jump, they sing... and they do that regardless of what's happening on the field. In fact, sometimes they will chant and dance more when we get a goal scored against us because they're trying to motivate the players. With a lot of other sports, when your team starts to do worse, the culture is that the fans sit down, stop cheering and sometimes even boo or leave. Fans see that as a negative so they react in a negative way. Whereas in soccer, the fans try to become more of a part of the game day experience in those situations and rally the players.

The experience that we provide is really driven a lot by our fans. They show up and they just want to be a part of the experience. If we win, that's just a bonus.

Soccer fans' loyalty is driven much less by wins and losses than other factors. In our fan surveys, the number one reason fans listed for not renewing their tickets was because of game times. On-field performance is not nearly as important to our fans as the experience when deciding to purchase tickets or attend games.

Chapter 1: Key Takeaways

1. Based on research conducted at 140 sports
    organizations, the number one factor athletics
    administrators believe contributes to attendance is
    whether or not the team is winning.

2. Data suggests that in college football, some of the
    winningest teams are experiencing the largest drops in
    attendance.

3. Even teams with the most loyal and passionate fan bases
    are losing fans.

4. Major League Soccer is a great case study for a league
    whose attendance seems to be least affected by the
    quality of play as there appears to be no correlation
    between winning/losing and attendance among MLS
    teams.

5. There are many examples of teams who have less-than-
    stellar win/loss records but still have high attendance.

②
DO DIFFERENT

Even if winning *is* the way to drive attendance, we as marketers have no control over a team's performance. As much as we might like to be calling the plays, that's not in our job description. We have to figure out other ways to engage fans and inspire them to attend our events.

One of the ways athletics marketers seem to be attempting to do that is by increasing content to engage their fans before, during and after games. Unlike winning, content is something marketers can control.

When I began my career in athletics marketing as a designer in 2001, the University of Oklahoma Athletics Department had just received approval to convert the position from part-time to full-time. Back then, most athletics departments either had part-time designers or no designers at all, even the top tier programs. Of course, this was before social media was a thing so the need for creative content wasn't nearly what it is today.

Fast-forward to 2018 and not only does virtually every athletics program in the country have a designer, some of them have entire *teams* of designers. They're charged with doing the type of creative work I was producing in 2001 plus hundreds of other pieces of content aimed at engaging fans, building the brand and, hopefully, increasing attendance at events. In addition, many programs have hired sport-specific designers to help with content creation for both marketing and recruiting.

Never before in the history of athletics has there been more content created, seen and shared. Yet attendance continues to drop. How can this be? The answer is simple. It's not just about doing more. It's about doing different.

> "You hear everyone say it: If the team wins, we'll have great crowds. I'm not sure I buy into that. I think that it takes great ticket sales, great marketing, great communications and teaming up with a great coaching staff. That's when you see perfect attendance. When you sit and rest on your laurels and expect fans to continue to renew their season tickets, and are not actively engaging them, that's when you have problems."
>
> **Martin Salamone**
> *Senior Associate Athletic Director*
> *for Sales, Marketing & Revenue Generation*
> Vanderbilt University

One Size Doesn't Fit All

So if winning is not a strategy for driving attendance and increasing content doesn't seem to be working, what *is* the right strategy? What *will* inspire attendance at our sporting events? Therein lies the problem.

There is no one-size-fits-all solution for sports marketing, but for years collegiate athletics marketers have been looking at what other organizations are doing and applying that prescription to their own situation. That doesn't work because even though you may have the same symptom (empty seats) as another team or organization, it doesn't mean you have the same disease or same *cause* of the symptom.

Marketers should be following the same path to solutions as physicians do when treating patients. When a patient walks in and complains of a headache, the doctor doesn't say, "Oh, I had another patient one time with a headache. Here's what you need to do to fix it." No, they ask questions. Then they ask more questions. They examine the problem and if it persists, they run tests until they figure out what the root of the problem is. Once they understand what they're dealing with, they develop a plan to solve it. Many times, they have to adjust their plan throughout the process to adapt to changes. Sometimes they treat the problem and it comes back so they have to develop a new approach. But in every situation, they follow a very specific formula when diagnosing. They do the *research*. They develop *insight* based on that research. They use that insight to create a *strategy* for solving the problem.

Let me say that again. They do research. They develop insight. They create a strategy.

Spoiled Sports

This isn't groundbreaking information. Marketers in the corporate world cracked this code decades ago. But for some reason the athletics industry seems to be relying on goodwill to get fans to come to games. The fact is, we're spoiled. For nearly a century, athletics events were truly the only game in town. Travel wasn't as easy as it is today. We didn't have a thousand other forms of entertainment at our fingertips and our fans certainly couldn't watch every sporting event in the world on a device in the palm of their hands.

The problem isn't getting better. It's getting worse. And it's going to keep getting worse until we start treating our product the same way every other industry treats their products. We need to research our audiences, develop insights into their behavior and create a strategy for selling our product to that market.

The following chapters are going to take you through a winding road of what we as sports marketers are doing, why it's not working and what we can do to fix it. The first part of the book outlines a theoretical approach to a new method for sports marketing but there are plenty of tangible ideas toward the end that can help you execute a more effective marketing plan.

Brad Wurthman
Senior Associate Athletic Director
for External Operations
Virginia Tech

I have more faith in the people who work in our business than to say, "Well we'll just leave it up to the kids to win games and then that will justify our jobs." We have too many smart people in our business who have too many great ideas and have too much creativity to just leave it up to something that's out of our control. When I think about it, we are not your standard consumer packaged good. We are not Procter & Gamble, we're not trying to convince you on a perceptual map that Old Spice Body Wash is what you should use instead of Dove. We already have the love affair and emotional side covered when it comes to marketing. Our job is to deal hope. I remind our staff all the time: We are dealers in hope.

When things aren't going perfectly, we remind fans that brighter days are ahead. But we can't just sit around and wait until those days arrive. And conversely, when everything is great, we need to be throwing fuel on the fire. You can't stop because you're winning – you have to double down on success. The best part about what we do - the most exciting part I should say - is to sell when you're losing because anybody can sell when you're winning. If you can sell when you're losing then you can make a difference. Our job is to capture lightning when it strikes. If we do our jobs properly, if we sell when we're losing, we've built the bottle. Then when lightning strikes you're ready to catch it. Always build the bottle, occasionally catch the lightning.

You can't sit and wait because if you do it may never happen. Your team might never start winning. Or if they do, it might be too late. If you haven't planned out what you can do you're at the mercy of so many other factors. Sell as many as you can when you're still undefeated, which means before the Labor Day weekend.

How? You sell one ticket a hundred ways. Unfortunately what happens in our business is this assumption that you can sell 100 tickets one way and winning is the only answer. Go sell groups, go sell packages, go sell single game tickets. It's not okay to sit back and say, "When we win they'll come." Especially now.

It's not okay if we assume that the person who sits at home to watch us will come when we start winning. The person who sits at home is not coming unless we make it the place to be, unless we create the perception of hope. It's the people who want to be involved in community that maybe don't care if you win or lose. It's the kids in your community. It's the other people who want to be involved but don't really know how. And it's our job to go find them and give them an entry point.

Chapter 2: Key Takeaways

1. The current trend for trying to increase engagement and attendance is to drastically increase the amount of content fans see from an athletics organization.

2. Attendance continues to drop at a drastic rate despite this increase in content marketing.

3. It's not about creating *more* content. It's about creating the right content.

4. The only way to know how to create the right content is through research, insight and strategy.

3

THE PLAYERS

If you go to any athletics facility in the country you're going to see fans there. You'll see 3,000 fans in a 6,000 seat arena. Or 40,000 fans in a 50,000 seat stadium. Unless it's newly formed though, every team has that core group of fans. The problem most programs face isn't having an empty facility, it's closing the gap between two-thirds and completely full while avoiding attrition among the fans they already have. For most programs, narrowing that gap can result in hundreds of thousands of dollars or more in revenue.

This book is about filling our seats by bringing fans to our stadiums and arenas. So as you read forward about methods and tactics to drive attendance, don't think in terms of the fans who are already coming to your games – think in terms of appealing to those who are not.

In the discussion of driving attendance to sporting events, there are three major players: opponents, fans and motivators. It's important to understand each if you want to develop a marketing strategy that actually works.

Opponents

If you're reading this book, chances are you're working in sports marketing and therefore you're in some way affiliated with a sports team. Whether it's a professional team, college team, Olympic team or some other type of athletics organization, we can all agree that the singular goal of our teams is to win. They're all going after some sort of trophy, be it the world/national championship trophy, conference/divisional championship trophy or the rivalry trophy. And it can only be achieved by winning games. There's no way for our teams to go *around* their opponents to victory. The only way to achieve that goal is to go through them. To defeat them.

As marketers, our version of the trophy is a full stadium or arena. Sure, we have other goals to accomplish and they're not all related to putting fans in seats. But a full stadium/arena solves a lot of our problems. It not only increases ticket sales revenue, it also increases sponsorship sales revenue, concession sales revenue and apparel sales revenue. It drives ticket demand which affects fundraising tied to ticket sales (on the collegiate side) and it even creates an atmosphere that helps the team win. Point being, if we can put butts in seats, all of our other problems either go away or at least become more manageable.

Just like the teams we're marketing though, we have opponents – things standing in our way that prevent us from achieving that full arena. We can't go around our opponents. We have to go through them in order to defeat them. For the teams we support, the opponents are obvious. They know exactly who they're trying to defeat on the field of play. But who are *our* opponents when it comes to marketing to fans?

Other Teams. Maybe you're in a market like Raleigh, NC, where there are three major universities within a short drive all trying to draw new fans to their stadiums and arenas. Or perhaps you're a program like SMU or USC that's located in an area that offers a *lot* of professional and non-professional options for sports fans. Even if you're out in the boondocks without another team in sight, today's media makes it easy for fans to tune into other teams from a distance. Like it or not, all sports teams are competing with one another for fans. And those with physical proximity to another team (college or professional) must work harder than ever to get fans to their own stadium.

Other Entertainment. Let's face it: your fans have a lot of other options for entertainment. Depending on the area you're in, this list may include going to the lake, playing golf, going to the movies or the zoo, etc. The alternate form of entertainment that appeals most to your fans at any given time will depend on a myriad of factors such as their life stage, their disposable income, what their friends or family enjoy doing, and the weather. This opponent is more mercurial than other teams, because options for other entertainment are constantly changing in most markets.

The Couch. Possibly the biggest competitor that defeats us on a regular basis is the couch. Unfortunately, even our most passionate fans often choose to stay at home and watch the game where the tickets are free, the beer is cheaper, the seats are cushier and the air conditioning (or heat) offers a far more comfortable environment. Considering that virtually every sporting event is televised now, getting fans off their couches and through the turnstiles is an uphill battle.

So which opponent is your greatest threat? It depends on what type of fan you're talking about.

For instance, the couch is your biggest competitor when it comes to fans who have an existing affinity for your program. They're going to watch the game no matter what, it's just a matter of where. When it comes to fans who lack that affinity, those other forms of entertainment are defeating you. How can we turn the tables on those opponents and give ourselves the advantage when it comes to attracting fans? Well, first we have to understand the four types of fans.

Fans

Old Hat has done extensive research consisting of surveys and data analysis on sports fans from all over the United States. Through that research we have determined that there are four basic types of fans: Die-Hards, Casual Fans, New Fans and Fair-Weather Fans.

Die-Hard Fans. Die-hard fans are the lifeblood of your organizations. They're at every event, tailgating beforehand and sitting in the same seats that have been in their family for generations. They have a closet full of fan gear, they visit your website frequently and they listen to sports talk radio to get the latest information on your team. They eat, sleep and breathe your program and almost nothing can change that. For the most part, they come to you and they consider attending games a privilege (or in some cases, maybe even a right).

Casual/Consistent Fans. Our research has identified two groups (Casual and Consistent Fans) that share enough characteristics to group together. These fans have an existing tie to your organization, typically because they attended your university or grew up in your city watching your team(s) play. They have a few team shirts in their wardrobe and they attend at least a few of your events every year if/when they can. They love you and chances are, they're going to watch the majority of your games. However, watching from home is a real possibility with this group. Between the cost of tickets and the comfort of home, "the couch" defeats you with this group regularly.

New Fans. There's a wide spectrum that makes up this group, which means they're harder to define and target. For professional teams, this group consists mostly of those new to the market or prospective fans that just aren't aware of what you offer. For universities, this group primarily consists of new students. The freshman class at an average sized Division I university can expect approximately 5,000 (some much more, some much less) new students coming in each year. While some new students may already be die-hard fans, most won't be – which means you have four years to get them there. That's a prime opportunity.

Fair-Weather Fans. No one wants to admit they're a fair-weather fan but there are far more of these than we'd like. This is the group that only comes to games if you're a top team in the league. They wear your gear when you're winning but don't touch it if you're losing. They'll show up if there's a big-name opponent coming to town but only if the weather is nice and their friends are going too. You might see these people come to a tailgate beforehand and then just go home or to the bar during the game, or not watch it at all. This group is unpredictable because you can never tell what might make them decide to come to an event. They'll claim you're their favorite team but they'll never be season ticket holders, donate to your program, be able to name a single player or remember what your record is.

Motivators

Now that we've defined the types of fans you'll encounter and the types of opponents that are standing in your way, let's talk about the psychological motivators that compel fans to decide either *to* attend or *not to* attend. The primary motivators that affect a fan's decisions are different for each type of fan. Some factors can be influenced while others are beyond your control. Based on this, we can divide the four groups of fans in half.

The Sore Spot

There are two groups of fans that fall into what I call the sore spot: the area where you will see the least return on your marketing investment. These fans tend to fall at the far ends of the enthusiasm spectrum. They either already love you or they're unapologetically fickle, and throwing marketing dollars at them isn't going to make much of a difference in changing their minds.

Fair-Weather Fans

If any group is heavily affected by our win/loss record, it's these people. They want to see a winning team play a big name opponent. So if you have that going for you, great. But even then these fans can be sidetracked by virtually anything. If their friends decide not to go, if they are too tired, if they have a nasty hangnail… the list of things that sway their attendance decision is virtually infinite. In many ways, they're the sports equivalent of people who make shopping decisions purely on price. They simply aren't brand loyal and you can't make them be. You will never convert them to a die-hard fan, so don't waste your time or money trying to do so. Instead, treat them the way they treat you: opportunistically. When they want to come, sell them a ticket. But when they don't return, don't worry about it. There's nothing you can do about it. Most of the time you can just forget about these guys. If you reach out to them, only do so when you have money to burn and can inform them of something that's likely to impress them (like a big-name opponent).

Die-Hard Fans

At the opposite end of the spectrum from fair-weather fans, we have the die-hard fans. While fair-weather fans can be motivated to *not* attend by anything and everything, the die-hards are motivated *to* attend by anything and everything. These people are the core of your fan base. If they hear Seven Nation Army come on the radio, they start thinking about hearing it at the football stadium and they get psyched about the upcoming season. If they see a basket at the craft store, they think about your hoops team and they flip on sports talk radio to get some updates on the latest recruiting class. These fans are totally bought in. They *might* miss your event for a funeral, the birth of their child, or if their niece breaks all rules of decorum and schedules her wedding on a game day, but otherwise they'll be there cheering you on. This group loves you and is *looking* for reasons to come back. While it's important to maintain and manage your relationship with them, they aren't the best bang for your buck when it comes to driving attendance. If you're trying to get from 45,000 fans in your stadium to 55,000 fans, you're not going to do it by marketing to die-hards. So keep your investment here low (just enough to keep them happy) and focus instead on the groups that can help you move the needle.

The Sweet Spot

If you truly want to improve attendance, spend the bulk of your marketing time and money on the two groups that are most likely to respond to your efforts. Not all fans are created equal, and the fans in these two groups hold the most potential to become consistent attendees.

Casual Fans

With this group, you've basically won half the battle before you even begin. Casual fans already love you, so you don't have to convince them how great your team is. However, you do have to give them a reason to actually come to the game instead of watching it from someplace else. The key is to figure out what's holding them back. Maybe they're concerned about ticket cost. Maybe it's hard to get to the games. Maybe they're just apathetic about the stadium experience because you haven't shown them how much better it is than watching from their couch or a bar. Whatever it is, you have the power to convince them otherwise. They've already got fire in their bellies for your team, so find a way to stoke that fire and get them to the game. You'll want to focus on rewarding this group's passion and converting it to greater in-person attendance. Casual fans are by far the largest group of potential seat-fillers out there. There are probably thousands of graduates in and around your campuses that already have a tie to your university. There may be millions of people who have grown up in your cities watching your pro teams play from a distance and seeing your logo on everything in town. No group of could-be-attendees is bigger or easier to influence than casual fans.

New Fans

For new fans, the problem is a lack of affinity for your program. People who have relocated to your area or new students at your university tend to have limited knowledge of your team and what your game day experience offers. They might love sports. They might be loyal people looking for a great entertainment option they can be passionate about. But if we don't create that affinity within them, they're going to find something else. That means you need to educate them about what you offer and encourage them to give you a chance. And what we're currently doing obviously isn't working because attendance is down across the board, nowhere more than in the student sections.

As I write this, the Atlanta Hawks have the lowest average attendance in the NBA. They average about 14,500 fans per game in an arena that holds 21,000 fans. Last year 90,000 people moved to Atlanta, growing its population to more than 5.7 million residents. That represents 90,000 new opportunities to create affinity. Miami's numbers are similar. Around 80,000 people are moving to Miami annually. The area boasts a GDP growth higher than the national average and its business growth is 8th in the nation. Yet the Marlins averaged 16,000 fans shy of capacity in 2017. I don't mean to pick on the Hawks and the Marlins. They are only two of *many* professional teams that have more than enough new residents moving in but aren't able to bring those fans through the gates.

And what about collegiate athletics? There is no industry in the world that has the advantages collegiate athletics has in regards to creating brand loyalty for our product. If we're failing to get students to our events and are unable to convert them into lifelong consumers of our product, we should be ashamed of ourselves.

Here's Why

Step outside of your current mindset for a moment and imagine that you just inherited a hypothetical shoe company. The company has been around for more than a hundred years and has a storied past full of success. Literally hundreds of thousands of people have worn your shoes over the years and they're quite passionate about them. You have a very loyal group that buys your shoes no matter what and they brag about your shoes constantly. They're even known to wear t-shirts advertising your brand on almost a daily basis, doing your marketing for you. All you have to do is keep making decent shoes and they're on board for life. However, those customers will eventually die or maybe they'll move somewhere your shoes aren't available. So you'll lose a few here and there. Plus, you want to *grow*. You sell a million pairs of shoes every year but you *make* 1.2 million pairs of shoes. You want to be selling at least that many. Well, I have great news: in this hypothetical scenario you also have access to thousands of new, young potential customers every year. Better yet, these potential customers are actually going to come to your world headquarters where you are going to teach them the history of your company, teach them songs about your company and surround them with your company's brand on a daily basis for four years. They'll see your logo on every trash can and building they pass. You're also going to be able to give them free or reduced-cost shoes the entire time so you can show them just how great your shoes are. And as if that's not enough, they're going to pay *you* thousands of dollars over the course of these four years.

I think you'd argue that in this scenario, you have absolutely no excuse not to turn these people into loyal purchasers of your product. But this is *exactly* what we get in collegiate athletics. Thousands of new students come to our campuses every year, pay us for the right to be there and then are completely immersed in our brands for four years. Even better, they're at the age when they are forming their identity and becoming who they're going to be for the rest of their lives. Thirty-and-forty-somethings are already set in their ways but 18-22 year olds are young enough to be impressionable and old enough to make buying decisions and develop brand loyalty. There is no age more perfect for turning consumers into loyal champions for our brands. Can you imagine what Nike would pay for this kind of brand exposure?

Nike University

Rather than leave it up to the imagination, I decided to find out. It's a really difficult question to answer but I had conversations with 6 different people who have spent their careers working in sports sponsorship sales on both the collegiate and professional level. Combined, they account for more than 100 years of experience in this field so if anyone is qualified to help me think through this scenario, it's these guys.

The question I posed was this: If Nike came to you and wanted to buy the rights to a university purely for the purposes of brand exposure to that university's student population (based on an average class size of 5,000 students), what would the value of that be? The Nike brand would completely replace the university's brand. Instead of chanting, "Rock, Chalk, Jayhawk," (for instance), they'd chant, "Just Do It." Instead of learning "Boomer Sooner," they'd learn a song touting the strength and power of Nike. They'd learn the storied history of the Nike organization and walk past a statue of Phil Knight every day. And after four years, they'd spend the rest of their lives with a Nike diploma on their walls and listing their time at Nike U. on their resumés.

While the response to this question was slightly different from each person, each could easily be summed up with something like, "Oh my gosh! That's a really hard question to answer. It's almost incalculable."

Obviously no one could give me an exact answer because nothing like this has ever been done. It would take weeks or months to try to wrap one's head around the value an agreement like this could provide. One way we attempted to arrive at a dollar value was to calculate how much each student would go on to spend on athletics apparel after college. Conservatively, we assume that each student would spend $100/year on athletics apparel for the rest of their lives. Not every student would be totally committed to Nike, of course. But some would spend exponentially more than that so we think $100/year per student is a fair assumption. That means that if they live to be 72, each class of students will account for more than $25 million in revenue for Nike. That's huge, in and of itself.

What one of my experts pointed out though is that this doesn't even consider the brand loyalty that would come out of the family and friends of each student over the course of *their* lifetimes. Each student's children, spouses, parents and siblings would undoubtedly be affected by the immersion in the Nike brand. As one of my sources stated, "I worked at an Under Armour school when my son was little and that's still the only brand he'll wear six years later."

In the course of my conversations on this topic, no one felt they could commit to an exact value. They'd say it was priceless. They'd say it's incalculable. When pushed to provide a dollar figure though, the lowest estimate I heard was $50 million per year. That's what Nike would have to pay every year to get what we get without spending a dime. That seems like a lot of money. But that was just their estimate for a *small* university. My conversations went further and dug deeper and as we started talking through all of the value a corporate brand could actually get out of something like this, the numbers grew to $100 million, $300 million and even $500 million dollars *per year* of value in brand exposure.

Think about that. A university athletics program receives

between fifty and five-hundred *million* dollars in brand exposure every year among their student population alone. Athletics departments receive what a company like Nike or adidas would be happy to pay in excess of $100,000,000 every year for. And we not only get it for free but these young, impressionable minds are actually paying *us* the whole time. We have every benefit imaginable in building our brands with our students. If we aren't getting them to our events and turning them into eventual die-hard fans, we are *doing something wrong*.

Our job as marketers is to somehow ignite the existing affinity in casual fans and create affinity in new fans. That's what marketing is! The problem, historically, has been that athletics has treated its product as if it's somehow different from every other product out there. We treat our product as if it's a privilege to consume it. We publish our schedules and expect people to show up. Yes, we do other things. But obviously they're the *wrong* things or we wouldn't have the attendance problems we have. We have to get over the idea that we're special and start marketing our product no differently than Ford markets automobiles or Wrigley markets gum.

Fan Commitment Level	LOW ←————————————→ HIGH			
Fan Type	Fair-Weather	New	Casual	Die-Hard
Group	Sore Spot	Sweet Spot	Sweet Spot	Sore Spot
Marketing Focus	Ignore or Impress	Create Affinity	Activate Affinity	Maintain & Manage
Marketing Emphasis	Low/None	High	High	Low

Chapter 3: Key Takeaways

1. Sports teams have opponents they must defeat in order to achieve their goals. As marketers, we too have opponents that are defeating us for fans' attention (i.e. other sports teams, other forms of entertainment, the couch, etc.).

2. There are four primary types of fans we can market to: Die-hards, Casual, New and Fair-weather.

3. These fans can be broken into two groups: Sore Spot and Sweet Spot.

4. Sore spot consists of die-hards and fair-weather fans. Their behavior is difficult to affect because die-hards will attend all games without fail and fair-weather fans are inconsistent and unpredictable.

5. Sweet spot consists of the two types of fans whose behavior we can affect through marketing: casual and new. The way to do that is through *activating* existing affinity with casual fans and *creating* affinity with new fans.

6. Universities receive millions of dollars worth of brand exposure with their student bodies at no cost and have an unbelievable opportunity to convert those students into loyal fans.

4

EMOTIONAL, RATIONAL & FACTUAL

We've talked about the types of fans and what motivates them. We've outlined our opponents and how they defeat us. Next we'll dive into the various types of marketing styles we use and how effective each is (or isn't) for each of the different types of fans.

There are basically three categories of marketing appeals. You can label them a number of ways but for our purposes we'll call them Emotional, Rational and Factual.

Emotional marketing is what we see used most prevalently in athletics. Examples of this would be a poster featuring an athlete ripping their jersey open with smoke and fire in the background. Or simply a print piece featuring a group of athletes looking menacingly at you while holding whatever ball their sport features. This type of marketing also consists of the hype videos and commercials that showcase big hits, slam dunks, touchdown passes and last-second goals, all followed by massive celebration. This is the kind of marketing that really gets your heart pumping. Emotional marketing doesn't have to just be all about the hype though; it can just as easily tug at the heartstrings. Examples of this emotional style include videos talking about how your support impacts student-athletes' lives and or commercials highlighting your favorite team's involvement in the community. Whether it's through high-impact visuals or feel-good messaging, emotional marketing is aimed at drawing you in by appealing to your heart.

Rational marketing, on the other hand, is all about highlighting the rational reasons one should buy a product or, in our world, attend an event. If emotional marketing appeals to your heart, rational marketing appeals to your mind. In athletics, this would include things like focusing on ticket cost/value of entertainment, pregame activities, halftime entertainment, family atmosphere, ease of attending, etc. The list is endless here and is determined by the unique aspects of each organization's game day experience.

Factual marketing is really just what it sounds like: presenting the facts in a very straightforward way. This would be telling people your game time and who your opponent is. We see a lot of this on social media, on signs on campus or outside the stadiums or in that old standby, newspaper ads (although hopefully most of you aren't throwing money away on those anymore). If all you're doing is listing ticket cost rather than focusing on value, that could be thrown into the factual marketing category as well. Ultimately though, it's just the facts: this is the product, this is where you get it and this is how much it costs.

Connecting to Fans

If those are the three basic types of marketing styles we can employ, we need to look at how each appeals to the different categories of fans we've defined.

Emotional
Emotional marketing, without question, is very appealing to die-hard fans. As a group that gets excited by virtually everything team-related they encounter, they are especially excited when they see those posters hanging in the local donut shop or the commercials full of the highlights they replay in their dreams every night. Emotional marketing also appeals to casual fans because they have an existing (though lesser) affinity for your team. New fans, on the other hand, are not great targets for emotional marketing because your team doesn't matter to them yet. While emotional marketing pieces may help demonstrate what you're all about and pique their interest, it won't be enough to get this group to take action. Fair-weather fans might like the emotional stuff. Or maybe they won't. But as we've determined, trying to appeal to this group of fans isn't the best use of your time anyway.

Rational

In addition to being affected by emotional marketing, casual fans can also be influenced by rational marketing. This is a group that is looking for a reason to attend your events, so make sure you're giving it to them. New fans are also a great target for rational marketing tactics. They have no affinity for your team but chances are they're looking for *something* to occupy their time. They might even love sports. This is your opportunity to convince them you're a better use of their time or money than Netflix. Die-hard fans may appreciate a rational appeal as well, but it's just icing on the cake because they're already planning to be at the game. Fair-weather fans don't care about rational reasons to attend. If the team is good, their friends are coming and the weather is nice, they'll be there. Otherwise, we can smack them with rationality all day long and it's not going to affect them. It's just noise as far as they're concerned.

Factual

New fans are the group that can be influenced the most by factual marketing tactics. Die-hard and casual fans already know the facts. They know who we're playing and they know when the game is. We don't need to remind them. If they don't know, they'll Google it. New fans, on the other hand, don't know what they don't know. Seeing that campus sandwich board or social media post might just be the nudge they need, as long as you've done something to get them interested in coming to the game in the first place. Factual marketing can also help you appeal to fair-weather fans if you want to spend time and money doing so – just don't hold your breath because they might change their minds.

Chapter 4: Key Takeaways

1. The three basic types of marketing are Emotional, Rational and Factual.

2. Emotional marketing tactics only appeal to two types of fans: die-hards and casual.

3. Rational marketing tactics appeal primarily to casual and new fans.

4. Factual marketing can be valuable for new fans and fair-weather fans.

5

THE SCIENCE OF EMOTIONAL MARKETING

It should be obvious to anyone working in sports that athletics organizations rely heavily on emotional marketing tactics. Whether it's commercials full of impressive three-pointers and quarterback sacks or athletes earnestly asking you to donate to or support their programs, sports marketing is all about playing on the emotions. But as we're seeing, it's not enough. Why?

The largest group of potential fans-in-stands is the casual fan group. Emotional marketing appeals to casual fans. Most of what we do in athletics is emotional marketing! So why in the world does attendance continue to drop? Why aren't these casual fans showing up in droves to attend our events?

Because emotional marketing tactics, by themselves, don't work. Plain and simple. As it turns out, there's a scientific reason for that.

Negativity

Over the course of hundreds of thousands of years, the human brain has evolved to do many things really well. One of those things is keeping us safe from harm when faced with a potentially dangerous situation. Thousands of years ago that may have meant something far different than it does now, but our brain still reacts the exact same way today as it did back then.

Let's say you're at a bar and you spill your beer on someone who's had a few too many already. This individual wants to fight and now you're faced with some negative stimuli. At this point, your blood starts pumping, your adrenaline soars and the amygdala part of your brain kicks in and literally takes over your decision-making ability. We've all been here before, whether it's in a bar fight or an argument with our significant other. We stop thinking rationally and we go into fight or flight mode. Maybe that means throwing punches or running out the door. Maybe it means screaming profanity or escaping both physically and emotionally by completely shutting down. Either way, we're not in control of our actions. As much as we might want to react one way – a rational way – we can't seem to control it.

Over time, of course, those emotions die down and we begin thinking rationally again. We begin thinking about the way we reacted to the situation and in many cases, we regret our decision to react that way. But it wasn't a decision. Our brains take over in those situations. While we can learn to control our responses, our brains always have the upper hand in this type of scenario.

Response to Negative Stimuli

 1. We face negative stimuli.

 2. The amygdala takes over.

 3. We start thinking irrationally.

 4. We make poor decisions.

 5. Emotions die down.

 6. Rational thinking returns.

 7. We (perhaps) regret the way we reacted.

Positivity

If we lose the ability to think rationally when faced with
negative stimuli, what happens when faced with positive
stimuli? Surprisingly, it's virtually the exact same thing.
We've all been there too. We're faced with something
overwhelmingly positive and our emotions get the best
of us. Our brain takes over, clouding our judgment. In
this situation, however, rather than throwing punches
or screaming profanity, we fall in love with whatever is
causing that influx of positivity. In many cases, we then act
irrationally – whether that means buying a product we don't
really need, getting into a relationship that's not good for us,
or doing things that are seemingly out of character. When
those heightened emotions wear off, we're often left with
regret.

Think About It

Marketers and advertisers figured this out about human
behavior years ago and they've been taking advantage of it
ever since.

We all face emotional sales and marketing tactics on a daily
basis. From the car dealership to the checkout stand, we're
in a constant battle with our emotions over what to purchase
and what to pass over. Even something as simple as seeing
that bag of M&M's at the cash register is positive emotional
stimuli. You're standing there impatiently waiting for your
groceries to be rung up. You're annoyed, you're hungry

and you've been walking around staring at food for a half hour. You want something – anything – to make you feel a little bit better. You look up and staring you in the face is a bag of chocolatey happiness. You start thinking about how good those M&Ms will taste and how much better you'll feel having eaten them. So you grab the bag, get it scanned, tear it open and wolf it down. No judgment, we've all been there. After a bit of time, of course, your emotions die down and you inevitably regret that decision to eat an entire bag of candy in 30 seconds. You saw the candy aisle but unless candy was on your list, you weren't buying it there. Why is that bag of M&Ms so hard to pass up at the last minute? It's because the checkout stand placement encourages an emotional, impulse decision. The candy company and the grocery store put it there because they know your state of mind when you're waiting to check out. They want you to make the decision quickly without having time to do one simple thing: think about it.

The most dreaded words to a salesperson are "I'll think about it." It's the last thing in the world any salesperson wants to hear you say. They don't want you to think about it because they know they'll lose you. When you take time to think about it, your emotions will die down, rational thinking will return and you probably won't make the purchase.

We see this all the time at car dealerships. They get you into that new car, driving down the highway, the new car smell wafting through the air. The salesman is right there with you talking about all the amazing features and how much better your life is going to be if you buy it. You start thinking about how you'll be the envy of your neighbors and how all the guys/girls will think you're dead-sexy driving that thing around. When you get back to the lot, the salesperson will do anything to keep you there. The one thing they absolutely do *not* want you to do: think about it.

My last and favorite example of this, believe it or not, is the state fair. We've all been to a state fair at some point in our lives and we've walked through the big building with the booths selling whatever new and amazing gadget will supposedly make your life a thousand times better. It should come as no surprise that the salespeople at these booths are actually highly trained individuals who spend years and years honing their craft. They're selling the fancy sprinkler head with so much passion you think they must have invented it. But last week they were selling the Potato-matic potato peeler one state over with that same passion. They're good at what they do because they know how to appeal to your emotions.

You're walking by a booth, minding your own business, when some charming individual leans out to ask you a simple question. If you answer, that's the first step in hooking you, regardless of the answer. They're friendly and engaging; they make you feel good by joking around and making you laugh. Then they start asking you questions about how you currently peel your potatoes. And somehow they have you questioning how you've lived your entire life up to this point doing it the way you've always done it. They start showing you their amazing new potato peeler and how it can do spiral cuts and waffle cuts and zig zag cuts and pigtail cuts (I made that one up). Your mind is blown and you imagine taking your potato casserole to the church picnic with spiral cut potatoes. You imagine how jealous Mrs. Johnson is going to be when she sees what you brought. You think of all the time you'll save in the kitchen peeling potatoes and all of a sudden, before you realize it, you've purchased the Potato-matic. On your drive home though, those emotions die down and you regret forking over $19.99 for one more thing you are going to stick in the drawer and never figure out how to use.

Regret kicks in as soon as you *think about it*. Which is why any salesperson will tell you that once they hear those words, they know they've lost you. If you tell them you'll think about it, they just move on to the next person and assume you won't be buying.

What That Means For Sports

You know emotional marketing tactics will appeal to casual fans and you're giving it all you've got. So why isn't it helping drive attendance? Because we give them time to *think about it*. When we rely so heavily on the emotion of sports to be the basis of our marketing, we only appeal to one potential group of fans. When we hook them with emotion alone, their decision to act isn't quick enough for our tactics to be effective.

Here's what happens: a casual fan walks past the poster featuring your athletes looking larger than life or sees the commercial with the big hits, slam dunks and amazing goals. They get excited. They think about how much fun it would be to go to the game with their buddies or take the family. They remember those great moments they used to have going to games. Then the commercial ends or that poster is no longer in view. And they *think about it*. Time passes and the emotion wears off and by the time the game comes around, the appeal of watching from a soft couch with cheap beer and an amazing HVAC unit drowns out the emotions that made them want to go to the game before.

So we employ a different tactic: outbound ticket sales teams. We have people call our list of former season ticket holders or single game ticket purchasers and talk them into purchasing again. These highly trained salespeople know exactly what to say and how to say it in order to paint a picture for these fans of why they cannot miss out on the opportunity to attend these events. They talk about supporting the athletes and how much fun it is to be at the games. They do the same thing the car dealers and state fair workers do and just like those salespeople, the one thing they don't want you to do is *think about it*.

Please don't misunderstand me here. I am in full favor of hiring ticket sales teams. They are a highly effective way to increase ticket sales and get people through the gates. So don't for one second think that I feel otherwise. However, in order for these ticket sales groups to be as effective as possible, we *must* use them in conjunction with the right kind of marketing so people won't do what the potato peeler purchaser does – throw the tickets in a drawer and never quite figure out how to use them. Unfortunately, what happens so often is that after the ticket purchase is made, the fan thinks about it and decides not to attend. Or they go to a game or two and give the rest of the tickets away to their fair-weather fan friends and family.

In order for ticket sales teams to be as effective as they can be, we have to create a marketing plan that makes fans *want* to attend. So when they get that call, it's not just the emotions fanned by the salesperson that's making them want to buy, there's also a rational basis for their decision that helps them feel good about it once the money is spent.

In addition to making our fans want to attend in the first place, we also have to make them want to return by giving them an unbelievable game experience. But we'll dig into that in later chapters.

Where Does that Leave Us?

I have worked in sports marketing for nearly 20 years and have run a company that caters to the athletics industry for 15 of those years. When I was working for the University of Oklahoma Athletics Department I designed every piece of print collateral for marketing, fundraising, sports information and academics. Since launching Old Hat, I have been a part of the creation of literally thousands of posters, commercials, radio spots, websites, hype videos, videoboard entertainment and every other form of sports marketing creative imaginable for more than 150 sports organizations. It could be argued that there's no one person in the country who has had their hands in more sports marketing creative than I have. And based on my experience, I can without a doubt say that we are spending virtually all of our time, money and effort on emotional marketing tactics. Everything I see in the sports marketing space is intended to be louder, cooler, more dramatic, more heartwarming or "pop" more than anything before it.

We are playing to people's emotions, which makes sense because sports is an emotional thing. People are emotional about their sports teams, especially the die-hard fans. But like I said, the die-hards are already coming to your events. It's the rest of your fan base you need to think about.

Don't get me wrong here. I love the emotional stuff. I've built a career around developing the most eye-popping sports marketing collateral around. Old Hat is great at creating hype videos and dramatic videos that either give goosebumps or make fans cry. That's what we do. But it's time for the industry to stop looking to those things as a way to drive attendance. Emotional marketing tactics have their place in sports marketing. They're icing on the cake for die-hard fans and help create a cool game experience for the casual and new fans we can get through the gates. What they do *not* do, however, is drive attendance. They don't appeal to the two groups of fans that are going to help us get from 45,000 fans at our games to 55,000 fans.

As an industry we have to start making our creative smarter, not cooler. We have to start delivering a message and telling a story instead of just trying to copy or outdo what the rest of the industry is doing. We have to stop competing with each other and start competing with our real opponents. We have to get it out of our heads that it's all about great *design* and realize that it's about far more than that. We have to stop marketing to the fans that are already coming and start marketing to those that aren't. Because guess what: the die-hard fans are going to love what we put out there no matter what. The rest of our target audience? Not so much.

Chapter 5: Key Takeaways

1. When faced with either negative or positive stimuli, the human brain thinks and acts irrationally. We can only begin thinking rationally once time has passed and emotions die down.

2. In emotion-based marketing and sales, allowing consumers to "think about" their purchase often results in no purchase.

3. Sports marketing that relies too heavily on emotional marketing strategies does not work because it allows fans too much time to "think about" purchasing/ attending.

6

A PERFECT WORLD

If die-hard fans are going to come no matter what, if the only thing predictable about fair-weather fans is that they will never turn into consistent consumers of our product, and if casual and new fans aren't responding to all the effort we put into emotional marketing strategies, what do we do?

First, forget about the die-hard and fair-weather fans. Don't market to them. Not because you don't need them, but because they're either already attending games (die-hards) or unlikely to ever attend games consistently (fair-weather). It's time to stop looking at these groups as potential contributors to attendance growth.

Second, create a strategic marketing plan to reach the fans that aren't coming to your events and target your marketing at them.

Strategic Marketing

We've all heard the term *strategic marketing* before. It basically means mixing the different types of marketing styles together into a set of messages that will appeal to the right people at the right time in the right place in the right way. Strategic marketing is difficult. It takes figuring out who your current consumers are and what drives them so you can target like-minded people to become new customers. It takes a deep analysis of your market to determine who you can target. It takes an understanding of how you can position your program to appeal to those groups along with what media to use and in what ways to use it. It requires you to figure out what is unique about what you're selling so you can position it properly for the available consumers in your market. It takes a lot of research and insight to create an effective strategy.

After deep and involved research, you might determine that your product should rely heavily on factual marketing augmented by equal parts of emotional and rational appeals. Or maybe you're selling something that has very little emotional appeal so you go big on the rational reasons to purchase and downplay the emotional aspects. Either way, you have to do your homework in order to come up with the strategy that's going to work for your unique product offering, market and target audiences.

Imagine trying to sell a washer/dryer set purely using emotional marketing tactics. High impact photography and videography showing how amazing the washer looks. A father and daughter sharing a heartfelt bonding moment while pulling clothes out of the dryer while soft music plays in the background. Great! But does it clean the clothes? Is it reliable? Has this brand won any awards? How much does it cost? Where do I get it? If you're selling a washer/dryer set, maybe it's best to focus more on the rational and factual aspects of the product. On the other hand, if you're a well-established washer/dryer brand with a high level of product awareness, maybe all you need to do is add some emotion to what people already know about your product.

The point is that with any product, the "right" strategy depends on a lot of different factors. What's right for one brand or product won't necessarily be right for another, even if we're talking about similar products. And no matter what you're selling, it's a mistake to rely too heavily on any single style of marketing. While you might use different tactics or media types to share different types of information, your marketing strategy has to hit consumers from all angles (emotional, rational and factual).

Example: The F-150

A great case study on this concept is the Ford F-150. If you pay attention to how Ford markets, you'll see that they're employing a strategic marketing message mix. They do it effectively and they do it big.

You're watching the Super Bowl and a commercial break

begins. Soft music interrupts the commentators' voices and the on-field action. You see a farm at sunset. A little girl walks with her father as their cattle graze in the distance. He lifts her up onto the tailgate of his F-150 where she can look at her daddy face-to-face. She smiles at him and puts her hands on the bristly whiskers of his face, bringing a warm smile to the hardened man. They nod as if to say that maybe it's time to be getting home but they turn and grab one last glimpse of the sunset before they go. Daughter has her arm around daddy's neck as the camera pans back to see three silhouettes break the sunlight as it shines brightly over the horizon. Those three silhouettes: daddy, daughter and the F-150. The commercial ends and everyone with a child is thinking about how much they want to be on a farm at sunset with their F-150 so they can have a moment like that. Or they're bawling because they're thinking about having had a moment like that (or wishing they had) with their own father. The Ford logo pops up on screen and in that moment, we love ourselves some Ford Motor Company.

But that's not enough, of course. And Ford knows that. So the next night when you're watching another nationally broadcast television show, targeted at a certain F-150-driving audience, there's another Ford commercial. This one talks about the payload capacity of the pickup. It shows the truck pulling a boat or carrying a load of gravel. They talk about how it's the most reliable truck on the road and that it gets great gas mileage. Finally, they throw in how many *Car & Driver* awards it has won and oh, by the way, the F-150 is the best-selling pickup of all time.

By this time, they've already roped you in with that emotional Super Bowl ad and created some brand affinity with you. Then they show you all of the rational reasons you should buy their pickup by allowing you to imagine yourself hauling rocks and pulling your boat. They give you some comfort by telling you how reliable it is and that it wins some awards you've never heard of. By this time, you're definitely feeling good about the F-150.

Another day goes by and you're watching the local news, which obviously only people in your area are going to be watching. Prime spot for a commercial about a local business, right? Maybe a car dealership? Sure enough, on comes a spot for Stockton Ford where you can get $3,000 cash back and 0% financing for a limited time on the 2018 F-150. They have every color in stock with every trim package available. All you have to do is come on down to I-420 and University Blvd. and pick yours out today!

See what they did there? They hit you *hard* with all three marketing styles: Emotional, Rational and Factual. They used three very different approaches for selling the exact same product. In a short period of time, you were introduced to all of the emotional, rational and factual reasons you should buy an F-150 and how to go about doing it.

And that's just a set of television spots – one piece of Ford's total marketing effort for the F-150. They're also using digital advertising, print advertising, outdoor, radio, social media, on-the-lot materials and various other tactics to help them reinforce their messaging. You can bet that the type of marketing selected for each tactic and media placement has been decided within the framework of a deep understanding of their target audiences and a well-planned marketing strategy. All of those key message points and different types of appeals come together to show you, the F-150 target audience, why you need their product or why you made a great decision by choosing their product already.

In a perfect world, that's how every product would market itself. But we don't live in a perfect world, do we? We can't spend millions of dollars on multiple commercial shoots targeting different marketing styles. We can't spend the $2.4 billion each year on media like Ford does.

What Do We Do?

So if we need to adjust our marketing strategy away from focusing so heavily on emotion and we can't afford to spend the time and money on all three styles of marketing, what do we do?

Focus more on the rational.

Our target groups for increasing attendance are casual fans and new fans. Only one style of marketing appeals to both of those groups: rational. So what we have to do is develop a rational messaging strategy to target those fans. That's not to say that we abandon the emotional or factual aspects of our product. What we're selling is still highly emotional and it's still important to make sure consumers know how and where to purchase tickets. However, the main focus *must* be on the rational reasons casual and new fans should attend our events.

What are those rational reasons? I have no idea. And neither do you. Not until you do the necessary research and develop insights based on that research. Only then can you create a strategy for increasing attendance. Once that strategy is defined, you have to go all in on it. Roll it out across *all* of your marketing materials and make sure those materials are getting in front of the people you've identified as the prime new targets to attend your events.

I'll spend some time on specific research tactics later in the book and provide some tangible ways you can get the information you need to develop a strategic marketing plan. For now, the important thing is acknowledging that:

1) The way most of us are trying to reach our fans isn't working.

2) We're focusing too heavily on emotional tactics.

3) We need to be more strategic in our approach.

4) The only way to develop a good strategy is through research and insight.

David Finnegan
Brand Content Manager
Ford Motor Company

It's important with your marketing that you cover all your bases. I typically think of it like a funnel. At the high end where the funnel is the widest, there are people aware of your product but might not be in the market for it. So you really need to keep your brand top of mind with your audience and continue to nurture their beliefs in you and positive feelings toward your brand. The Super Bowl spots are a great example. The latest Super Bowl ad showed a series of relatable situations people get in where they feel stuck. There was a man sitting on a stopped ski lift, a man trying to get out of a wet suit and someone stuck on the side of the road with a flat tire. All relatable situations where people feel stuck. As the story unfolds you see the moment when each individual broke free and became unstuck. It highlighted that exhilarating feeling you get when you're free. And that was how we communicated the Ford brand. We help people find new ways to move freely through life.

The goal is a high level awareness of the brand. As you move further down the funnel, you find people who are in the market for an automobile and need more specific information about the car – like how much cargo room it has, how many miles per gallon it gets or if it has a roof rack. Even further down the funnel you have people that are actually ready to make the purchase and need marketing information that communicates the rebates or prices and where to purchase it.

So you need a mix and it's not necessarily an even mix. You wouldn't do a third, a third and a third but because you have people at different stages of the buying process, your marketing has to cover all areas of that funnel.

Chapter 6: Key Takeaways

1. Stop focusing your marketing efforts on die-hard and fair-weather fans and start focusing it on casual and new fans.

2. Strategic marketing involves figuring out the right mix of emotional, rational and factual marketing based on your target audience.

3. Companies like Ford employ all styles heavily so as to cover all bases. We typically cannot afford to do so.

4. Considering that emotion-based marketing doesn't work on the types of fans we should be targeting, we should focus away from emotional and move toward a more rational based marketing strategy.

5. Only through research and insight can we figure out the rational reasons our target audience might attend our events.

"You have to make sure you have the best possible experience from start to finish. So often we focus on what we're going to do during a timeout or when the cheerleaders are going to come out. And those things are important. But you better have every aspect of that fan experience dialed up and that starts from when they buy a ticket to when they pull into their driveway that night after the game. It's making sure you have clean restrooms and making sure the ticket takers are friendly. Those are the things that keep people coming back because it can enhance their experience at the game. Winning and losing is a part of that experience. But if they feel good about everything else that happened, you can potentially cover up the product on the field."

Craig Pintens
Athletic Director
Loyola Marymount University

THE GAME DAY EXPERIENCE

Now that we know, at least in a theoretical sense, what needs to change about our marketing approach in order to drive attendance to our events, let's talk about how to keep fans coming back. After all, you're not trying to increase attendance for just one game (or if you are, that's a completely different strategy). Your goal is to get new blood through the gates and give them such a great experience that they'll keep coming again and again.

There's a lot more to the game day experience than the game itself. Everything inside and outside the stadium, before, during and after the game, affects whether attendees have a good time or not. As an administrator, you have a certain level of control over some of these factors while others are out of your reach. Every organization is different and your level of control may differ slightly from others, but I've broken down some of the more common elements based on what we learned in Old Hat's 2016 survey of athletics administrators.

Group 1: Ultimate Control

Although you might have to get buy-in from others, an administrator is often the ultimate decision maker on most of the following items:

- *Videoboard* - The hype video that plays as the team enters the field, the kiss cams or the shuffle game your fans love – anything that plays on the videoboard to engage and entertain our fans.
- *Promotions* - Halftime promotions, throwing t-shirts out during timeouts, honoring a long-time season ticket holder, etc.
- *Pregame* - Tailgate areas, pregame student entertainment, fan fest outside the stadium, etc.
- *Other Entertainment* - Anything outside of the above listed elements aimed at entertaining our fans.

Group 2: Some Control

While you may be able to affect the elements on this list, it typically takes more time or can be a bit more difficult to make changes in this area.

- *Customer Service* - From ticket takers to

concessionaires, you can train them but ultimately you cannot monitor their every interaction.

- *Food & Beverage* - You can change providers and try to bring new items in for your fans but you don't cook the food.
- *Ticket Cost* - While not necessarily easy to change, the cost of tickets to enter your events is something you can influence.

Group 3: Potential to Influence

Here are three more elements of the game day experience that you likely have less control over but still have the ability to influence in small ways.

- *Cheer & Band* - You can tell them when to cheer and play, but you have little to no control over how good they are at it. Just like the teams on the field/court, the quality of their performance is beyond your control.
- *Premium Areas* - Fans love premium areas and while you can build or create new ones for them, that's not an easy or quick process. Sometimes you lack the ability to affect this at all.
- *Ease of Attending* – This is extremely difficult to measure, first of all. But through surveys you can figure out how people feel about this and make some adjustments.

Group 4: Beyond Your Control

Finally, there are some pieces of the game day experience you have absolutely no control over. Unfortunately, they're the two factors most athletics administrators think are the most important factors in driving attendance.

- *Quality of Play* - Some of you might have the ability to hire or fire coaches, but that's about the only way you can affect the quality of play. Even *with* that power, there are too many variables that are completely outside your control to be able to affect this.
- *Quality of Opponent* - Again, you might have the power to schedule a big name opponent but you can't control how good they are when they actually show up. Nor can you control how much effort they put forth. They might roll into town as a top ten team or they might roll in having just lost five in a row with an interim head coach at the helm.

What Really Matters to Fans

In conjunction with the 2016 survey Old Hat conducted with athletics administrators, we also held a brief survey of sports fans coast to coast. Some of the questions we asked were similar across the two surveys because we wanted to compare answers from sports fans with those of sports administrators. The results were fascinating.

When asked what they believed were the most important factors motivating fan attendance at games, athletics administrators cited these top three factors:

#1: Whether or not the team is winning
#2: What opponent is being played
#3: The social aspects of game attendance

When we asked fans the same question, here's what they said was most important to them:

#1: Experience of watching live game action
#2: Relationship with school/team
#3: Ticket cost
#4: The social aspects of game attendance

This should be amazing news to anyone working in athletics marketing. The top two reasons fans decide to attend live athletics events are two things that you have automatically built in to what you're selling! The third thing on the list is within your control and the fourth is the most controllable aspect of what you do. Social aspects of game attendance is what marketing is all about. Athletics events are by nature social events and our job as marketers is to amplify those social aspects through everything listed in Group 1 above.

The really good news is what *doesn't* appear at the top of their list. When it comes to choosing whether or not to attend games, what do fans care least about? Winning and opponents. Those things are ancillary.

Obviously a winning team and quality opponents are important to some fans. That goes without saying. But as you can probably guess, the two groups of fans that are motivated by these things the most are the same two groups whose behavior is hardest to affect and least important to increasing attendance: die-hards and fair-weather fans. Which two groups listed ticket cost and the social aspects of game attendance highest? Casual fans and new fans.

> "You have to try to create those mini-experiences designed to appeal to each of the different generations. You have to have the marching band playing the right amount during the games because that's what the Baby Boomers want but you also have to create the 'Instagramable' moments for the younger generations. There's no one magic bullet. You have to get really deep and create those micro-experiences that speak to each of those groups and then place them and time them strategically so you're reaching the right people with the right experiences at the right time."
>
> Brian Bowsher
> *Chief Marketing Officer*
> University of Washington

I can hear the collective sigh of relief coming from the entire athletics industry right now.

One survey with one data set might not be enough to prove this point though so I'll highlight another.

As a part of Old Hat's brand development engagement with the Mountain West Conference in 2018, we surveyed sports fans on a number of topics. The survey population consisted of three groups: communities surrounding Mountain West institutions, current season ticket holders at those institutions, and the broader national audience. Among other things, we asked participants to rate several factors in order of importance when deciding whether to purchase sporting event tickets. The options they were asked to rank were:

- Success on the field
- Seat location
- Quality opponents
- Ticket price
- Game experience

The national audience listed "game experience" and "ticket price" as the top two most important factors (in that order) influencing their buying decisions. They listed "success on the field" and "quality opponents" as the least important factors. This is great information and certainly provides some hard evidence against the idea that fans care most about winning and what opponent you're playing. But few of us are trying to sell tickets to a national audience so it's not all that helpful.

So what did season ticket holders have to say? They ranked "success on the field" second, significantly ahead of where the national audience did. However, the most significant finding was that season ticket holders still listed "game experience" as the #1 most important factor when deciding whether to purchase tickets.

The third group we surveyed was community respondents - people who live within driving distance of these universities and are not season ticket holders. This group of respondents was comprised of self-proclaimed sports fans who were not in the season ticket databases of the Mountain West institutions. So what did they list as the most important factors when making a buying decision? Game experience, ticket price and seat location. Least important: success on the field and quality opponents.

What can we learn from this? So much.

First, it should come as no surprise that season ticket holders or "die-hard" fans care more about the product on the field than the other groups. This has already been established in previous chapters. This group wants the team to win but as we've discussed, they are the group that can least help us grow attendance because they're already there. They're also least likely to be impacted by changes to our marketing efforts. However, it's important to note that this group cares most about the game experience. If you want to strengthen these relationships and keep this group coming back, that's where you should focus your attention. The good news is that you have a great deal of control over several factors that contribute to the game day experience.

What is most fascinating and most useful about these

survey results though is what we heard from the community members. Why should we care about these folks? Well, it stands to reason that they either hadn't attended any events in the past (because maybe they're new to the area) or had only attended using friends' tickets or made single game purchases (more like a casual fan would). That means this survey group represents the greatest target of opportunity as prospective casual fans and new fans. The things that motivate them are the things we have the most control over. And as luck would have it, the only two things we have zero control over are the two things they care least about.

Again, this is just one survey and one example. The results of the Mountain West research can't be applied to every other conference or any single university. The same goes for the strategies that are developed out of those insights. But hopefully this example and the data from the Old Hat nationwide survey have helped you see how research can help uncover insights that may change the way you look at your fan base and your marketing efforts.

Keep 'Em Coming

We can't control how our teams play and we can't control who or how good the teams are that they're playing. But we have a high degree of control over the one thing that matters to nearly all types of fans: the game experience.

Die-hards are the one group that might stop coming if the team isn't any good. But as the data shows, giving them a top-notch experience might keep them coming back even if the quality of product on the field isn't so great.

The casual fans and new fans are the two groups that care most about the things we can control and the least about the things we cannot. We've already determined that this is where we should be focusing our marketing efforts. Now we know that we should be doing everything we can to give them an amazing experience when we get them through the gates.

> "When you're winning, that's fine. People will show up. But how do you get them to come back whenever the team stops winning? You have to use that time to build a strong foundation and create loyalty with your fans because if you don't have that foundation, everything will fall apart when or if the team stops doing so well."
>
> Daniel Nunes
> *Assistant Athletic Director for Marketing & Creative Services*
> Southern Methodist University

Chapter 7: Key Takeaways

1. Once you get your casual and new fans to attend an event, you must provide them with a great game day experience in order to get them to return.

2. Based on input received in a 2016 survey of athletics administrators, we ranked the level of control we have over each of the various game day elements.

3. The top two factors administrators *think* fans consider when deciding to attend are quality of play and quality of opponent.

4. Fans did not list either of these factors as one of their top four reasons they decide to attend.

5. The elements of the game day experience fans find the most important when deciding whether to attend are all things we have some level of control over.

6. In another survey, the group most likely to contain casual and new fans listed game experience, ticket cost and seat location as the top reasons they decide to attend.

8

RESEARCH + INSIGHT + STRATEGY

Now that we know who we should be targeting (in a general sense) and what's most important to them in getting them to keep coming back, the big question remains: how do we go about creating a marketing campaign targeted at the right people at the right time in the right place? And then how do we make sure our game day experience is one that's appealing to those people?

The answer is simple: research + insight + strategy.

Now, don't confuse "simple" with "easy." It's not easy. But you will *never* win until you commit to doing the necessary research, gleaning insights from that research and developing strategies to defeat your opponents. Your peers down the hall have figured this out so there's no reason you can't do it too.

The Football Office

I wanted to get an idea for how much time our friends down the hall spend on research, insight and strategy for defeating *their* opponents, so I spoke with a good friend who has worked for a top football program for the past 20 years. For the sake of keeping the focus on the big picture rather than this particular program itself, I'll simply say it's a perennial top 25 college football program.

I asked my friend roughly how much time the program spends researching their opponents and developing strategies to defeat them. She told me they employ nine people on their video team whose full-time jobs are to break down film on opponents and themselves. In other words, nine full-time employees who spend 40 hours per week, approximately 48 weeks per year (I gave them 4 weeks off) on research and strategy. She also said they have 11 full-time coaches who take that research, develop insight from it and create a strategy around it. Let's say conservatively that these 11 coaches only spend 20 hours per week for 20 weeks of the year on these strategies (I'm assuming they spend the rest of their time coaching and on related efforts).

Nine people on the video crew spending 40 hours per week, 48 weeks per year on research. Eleven coaches spending 20 hours per week, 20 weeks of the year on insight and strategy. That equates to more than 21,000 hours per year spent on research, insight and strategy by this particular football program. Twenty-one THOUSAND hours! And they still lose sometimes!

You might doubt my math but I honestly believe my numbers are conservative. I think it's safe to say these coaches are actually spending a lot more time than that on insight and strategy, and these estimates don't take into account any graduate assistants or players who spend time on watching game film and studying playbooks.

How does that compare to the others sports we're trying to drive attendance to?

I also spoke to coaches of a Division I women's basketball program, two soccer programs and an FCS football program. How much time do they estimate they spend on research, insight and strategy? The answer is 700, 2015, 530 and 1050 hours, respectively.

So the coaches down the hall from you are spending somewhere between 500 and 21,000 hours on research, insight and strategy. How much time are you spending on those things?

I did a little research on that as well. I asked a number of people in athletics marketing how much time they spend on this and explained what I meant by it. The numbers were all over the place but two responses were notable. The first was from someone that I respect as much or more than anyone in the field of athletics marketing. He is one of the most forward-thinking people in the field and someone who understands the importance of marketing strategy. I knew his answer would be a benchmark for the industry and I doubted that anyone would have a number higher than his. I ended up being correct, as no one could top the estimated 160 hours that he thought he and his team spent doing the necessary research, insight and strategy to defeat their opponents.

If that one was notable for how high it was, the other was notable for how low it was. I spoke to someone who has worked in a marketing capacity at four or five of the largest and most successful collegiate athletics programs in the nation. When I asked him, on average, how many hours his team spent on this type of effort, his answer was zero. Zero hours per year doing the very thing all of the coaches for the programs he was marketing for knew *had* to be done in order to defeat their opponents.

I was beside myself when I got these responses. How could this be?! How are we not spending more time doing what everyone in the organization knows must be done in order to win?

The answer is obvious: there's simply not enough time. Anyone who has ever worked in athletics marketing can tell you so. As marketers, we don't have a team of people researching all of our opponents day after day, week after week, all year long. We can't spend 20 hours of our week pulling insight from that research and developing strategies on how to improve our marketing game. Why? Because we have 15 to 20 sports we're trying to market on shoestring budgets with an inexperienced and overworked staff…not to mention having to deal with the spirit squad, band and all the other administrative duties.

If you look at the average marketing team size for any large athletics organization, you'll be hard-pressed to find one with more than four or five people in it. Five people charged with doing for 15+ sports what would be tough to do for a single sport. Five people charged with doing for 15+ sports what their football office has 20 people doing for one sport. And I'll say it again… the football team does this and *still loses* sometimes.

So the next time one of your coaches complains about how many people are attending their events, ask them how much time they spend on research, insight and strategy for defeating their opponents. Then point out how often they lose. If you still have your job after that, ask them to give up one of their coaches so you can hire someone to do research and strategy for your marketing department.

It's Time for a Better Strategy

This industry has to change if we are going to reverse the downward trend of attendance at our events. First, we have to abandon this idea that winning is a strategy for increasing attendance. For one, winning doesn't affect attendance nearly as much as we think it does. But far more importantly than that, even if it did, we have no control over winning or losing. As marketers, we need to vow to never again breathe anything resembling, "If we'd just start winning, attendance would take care of itself."

Second, we have to stop thinking that our hard-hitting hype videos or exciting posters are going to do anything to actually drive attendance. We have to embrace the science of consumer behavior and realize that emotional marketing tactics aren't enough. The hard truth is that when we market this way, we're only effectively appealing to the one group that's going to come to our events no matter what.

Third, we have to embrace the idea that what we're selling is no different than any other product out there. Coming to our events is not a privilege for fans. It's another form of entertainment in a world where people have more options than ever before. We must treat our product no differently than Ford or Dr Pepper or Nike treats theirs.

Fourth, we must make sure that the thing most important to all types of fans - the game experience - is one they cannot forget. All of the marketing in the world is worthless if your fans feel like you've let them down once they get to the game. Fans aren't expecting a guaranteed win, but they do want a guaranteed great game day experience. Screw this up and you'll lose them forever.

Finally, we must invest in research, insight and strategy. We have to stop allowing ourselves to be asked to defeat our opponents without being afforded the same types of resources our coaches are given to defeat theirs.

> "Winning definitely can't be our marketing plan. Winning helps but we weren't hired to coach or worry about what happens inside the lines. What we're responsible for is what happens outside the lines. And we have to be able to provide more than a winning product in order to get them to keep returning to our venues."
>
> Sarah Muñoz
> *Associate Athletic Director for Marketing & Fan Engagement*
> Arkansas State University

Chapter 8: Key Takeaways

1. The only way to create the right marketing strategy to get fans to attend and the right game day experience to keep them coming back is through: research, insight and strategy.

2. Our sports programs are spending between 500 and 21,000 hours per year on research, insight and strategy to defeat their opponents.

3. On average, athletics marketers are spending between zero and 160 hours per year on research, insight and strategy.

4. We have to invest in being more strategic with our marketing if we want to reverse the trend of declining attendance in athletics.

9

PAYING FOR STRATEGY

I've given my *Winning is Not a Strategy* presentation at numerous conferences and summits in front of hundreds of athletics administrators, and the response has been overwhelmingly positive. But the one question I get most is: *How do we pay for strategy when it's not something our organization has historically included in its budget?* The concern is that it will be difficult to get this expenditure approved because it's not something the program "needed" in the past. It's a valid concern as research, analysis, and strategic advisement can be expensive when done properly.

The good news is that there are ways to get this paid for without it affecting you organization's budget at all.

Every fan that walks in the gates at an athletics event results in a certain amount of ticket revenue, obviously. They all paid for their ticket and sometimes even made a donation in addition to the ticket cost. The amount of money each fan accounts for before even walking through the gate is obvious. But what we aren't paying enough attention to is the amount of money we are making off of them *after* they're through the turnstile.

The two major areas where fans account for additional revenue are through concession sales and apparel sales. I wanted to find out how much each fan accounts for in each of these categories at various institutions so I called several friends in the industry to find out. One thing I learned is these additional funds are referred to as "per caps." I'd ask the question and the response was generally something like, "Oh, you mean our per caps?" Yes… your per caps. What are they?

Here's the problem: no one knew. I did finally speak with one individual from a major Pac-12 institution who was able to tell me that for concessions, it ranged from approximately $9 per fan at baseball up to $13 per fan at football. But again, this was for concessions only. Apparel sales was not being considered in these numbers.

According to an article published by bizjournals.com that highlighted the per caps for the football programs at every university in the SEC, the average football fan at a Texas A&M football game will spend right around $10 per game on concessions once they enter the stadium. Their listed average attendance is right around 100,000 fans per game

which is an extra $1m per game, purely on concessions.
Throw in an average of another $20 on merchandise and
you've climbed to an additional $3m per game in revenue
beyond ticket cost.

Not everyone can pack in 100,000 fans per game though.
Research does show that the revenue-per-fan at Texas A&M
is fairly average so even if you're only expecting 50,000
fans, that's an additional $1.5m per game in revenue from
concessions and merchandise. And this doesn't include a
dime that the local hotels are making off of you.

Athletics departments are already getting a share of the
concession and merchandise sales, of course. But the food
and apparel partners are still making a lot of money off your
fans. More importantly, they'd stand to make a lot more if
you had more fans coming through your gates.

Strategic marketing, if done properly, typically sees results
of at least a 10% increase in sales. So do the math on your
stadium or arena. Let's say you embark on an engagement
that could result in an increase of 5,000 fans per game.
Looking at the additional revenue-per-fan that your partners
will be making, that equates to an additional $150,000 per
game, or nearly $1m per season.

Let's scale it back a bit though just in case the idea of 5,000
more fans at your football games is a bit of a reach. If you're

Rizvic, Veneta. "Here's how much SEC fans will spend on college football this season."
BizJournals.com, St. Louis Business Journals., 31 August 2018, https://www.bizjournals.
com/stlouis/news/2018/08/31/here-s-how-much-sec-fans-will-spend-on-college.html

currently bringing in 6,000 people to your basketball arena and your per caps for that sport are $10 for concessions and $5 for apparel, a 10% increase in attendance would be 600 fans per game at $15 per fan, which is $9,000 per game. Over the course of a typical basketball season, that could result in an additional $135,000 in revenue for your concession and apparel vendors.

Obviously, all those extra dollars don't equal net profit. There are hard costs for your vendors and you're already getting a cut. However, the companies that provide your food, beverage and apparel are in the business of making money. They know that everyone who walks through the doors has the potential to bring them additional revenue. Additionally, all of the hotels and restaurants in your area are making money off *your* product as well and generally, you *aren't* getting a cut of that. The more fans you're bringing to town, the more money they'll make.

So how can you get the funds to do research, insight and strategy? Ask your vendors, partners and area merchants to pony up some dough. Most will jump at the chance to do whatever is necessary to bring more fans to the stands and invest capital into something that could bring such a substantial ROI.

Chapter 9: Key Takeaways

1. Every fan that walks through your gates equates to an additional $9 to $30 worth of revenue between concessions and apparel sales.

2. Every additional fan results in more revenue for your food vendors, apparel partners, local restaurants and hotels.

3. One way to help cover the cost for additional marketing assistance is to solicit investment from those organizations to help increase attendance, thus resulting in additional revenue for themselves.

13 THINGS YOU CAN DO NOW

Up to this point, this book has talked about sports marketing in a very theoretical way. But I wanted to also provide some practical tips that athletics organizations can implement immediately to begin taking steps in the right direction. Research, insight and strategy isn't rocket science. While there are firms you can hire to help you, that doesn't mean you can't get started on your own right away.

Number 1:
Decide What You Are Selling

A 2016 *Planet Money* podcast highlighted the economics of stadium vendors at Fenway Park. Based on seniority, each vendor gets to pick what they want to sell each night and what section they are going to sell it in. Hot dogs in the bleachers. Beer behind home plate. One by one, they all pick their product and section.

One might assume that the same vendors would pick the same products and sections nearly every time. But that's not how it happens at all. The vendors know they have to analyze everything about the game and the crowd in order to pick the right product and the right section to maximize sales. They strategize based on what time the game starts, what the temperature is outside, the demographic makeup of the available sections and multiple other factors before making their decisions.

The more tenured vendors know exactly which item and section to pick in order to maximize revenue, tips and commissions on any given day. There's the obvious stuff like picking water for hot afternoon games or hot chocolate for cold evening games. But there's a much more precise science to it than that. They know that in the high-priced seats, Diet Coke sells better than Coke. They can tell by the time of year, opponent and start time what the demographics will be of each section and they will adjust their selections based on this information. Some games will have a higher percentage of rabid fans than others. Some will have more out-of-towners. And the buying habits of these groups is different.

What fascinated me the most was that it's the individual salespeople who have to do the analysis and strategy in order to decide what they're selling. Nobody in the front office was

"At the end of the day, we're in the business of selling experiences and trying to create memorable moments. At Xavier, we try to deliver the same quality, family-friendly, entertaining experience across all six sports that we sell. That's the product we're selling. The particular ticket product – whether it's a single game ticket all the way up to courtside basketball tickets – the price point and the point of entry is different. So that's where you use analytics in terms of your prospecting and your pricing to find the right audience and market directly to who you think is going to buy that particular product. And I think that changes based on different schools or programs you're trying to market."

Brian Hicks
Associate Athletic Director for External Relations
Xavier University

making these decisions. In fact, the front office realized that they'll turn more of a profit if they leave the sales decisions to those who are in the trenches, analyzing every piece of the puzzle before they decide what they're selling that day.

It's important to recognize that in athletics marketing, we should be doing the exact same thing. We aren't selling the same product to the same people in the same section each time a ticket gets purchased. We need to be analyzing our demographics, checking the weather, looking at game time, etc. before we can decide what we're selling. We're not just selling an opportunity to witness an athletics event. It's not that simple.

For some fans, we're selling nostalgia for a time they came to events as a child. For others, we're selling an afternoon with their children. We're selling date nights and social gatherings and new experiences. And to maximize revenue, we have to analyze our market and the climate and only then decide what we're selling and to whom. You can't sell a product until you decide what the product is.

Number 2:
Decide What it Should Cost

A recent Wall Street Journal article about college football attendance pointed out that for the fourth consecutive year, the sport saw a sharp decline of fans in our stadiums. A 3.2% drop just last season and a 7.6% decline over the past four years.

What I found most interesting about the article though was the comments section. It was a wealth of information with candid responses from fans about *why* they're not attending. Here are a few comments that followed a common theme I saw throughout the entire section:

"It is just too damned expensive."

"The average fan is not even a consideration in pricing..."

"Pay obscene prices for tickets, parking, food, drinks..."

Bachman, Rachel. "College Football's Growing Problem: Empty Seats." *Wall Street Journal*, Dow Jones & Company, 30 August 2018, https://www.wsj.com/articles/college-footballs-growing-problem-empty-seats-1535634001

There were comments highlighting other reasons fans choose not to attend, but those seemed to be from people that aren't going to come no matter what. The comments from fans that appeared to have a desire to show up but had a legitimate complaint about why they aren't, all centered around cost.

We've seen fan-friendly pricing take hold at the concession stand, which is a great step in the right direction. But what about ticket prices? Are we truly considering the average fan when pricing our tickets?

Considering the impact and response from fans around the nation about fan-friendly pricing at the concession stand, it seems as though fans really want a more affordable way to attend sporting events.

It begs the question: How much is too much? What *should* face value of our tickets be? Could we be charging more? The answer to that question can be found in research and data analytics. It's a matter of looking at historical sales data, surveying ticket holders and former ticket holders, analyzing census data to see what people in your area can afford, and looking very closely at secondary market data to see what the true market value of your tickets is. You might be charging way too much. Or, you might be leaving money on the table.

The information is out there and accessible, you just need to do the research and use it effectively.

Number 3:
Data Analytics and Lookalike Modeling

For the past couple of years, the hot topic around the industry has been data analytics. There have been multiple times though when I'm engaged in a conversation with a client that goes something like this:

Client: *Do you do data analytics?*

Me: *Of course! But tell me what you mean exactly because data analytics can include a wide spectrum of things.*

Client: *I don't know what I mean. I just know we need data analytics.*

Everyone knows they need to be investing in data analytics in order to move the revenue needle, but a lot of times they don't even know what that means. Everyone wants their data analyzed but many athletics departments think they don't have any valuable data to analyze. That, or it's really old and disorganized and full of inconsistencies and redundancies so we're faced with spending hours and hours just cleaning the data, which is an expensive process in itself.

So what do you do if you: 1) think you don't have any usable data or 2) are faced with having to spend the next year having someone scrub your data before you can get to anything worth analyzing? Keep it simple.

The biggest mistake organizations make is thinking they

don't have enough data to pull usable information from. Even the most basic data can still unveil some really great insight.

Here's an example. Let's say all you have is a couple of years of ticket sales information. You don't have any information on these people other than their addresses because you had to mail their tickets to them. Yet that's some *great* data right there.

Just having zip codes allows you to map all ticket purchases or donations to specific areas and understand the behavior of people in that area. Simply knowing that will reveal which zip codes are full of people who like what you're selling and can afford it. Additionally, loyal fans in these areas are probably influential to their neighbors so ramping up marketing efforts in these areas is a great first step. This approach becomes even more powerful if you have addresses to go along with those zip codes. Sometimes zip codes encompass pretty large areas so mapping specific addresses will be that much more effective. Either way though, simply using the data you have from mailing tickets to people is useful.

Taking it a step further, you can then analyze census data from those zip codes to determine the demographic makeup of those areas. You can find out household income, marital status and a wealth of other data that is available through the multiple online resources for this type of information. Analyzing this information will most likely provide 2-3 different groups and you can then use lookalike modeling to identify other areas with high concentrations of these demographics that are currently *not* purchasing tickets. Now that you've decided what you're selling and how much it should cost, you can create a marketing campaign that highlights what is appealing to these groups and target them in the areas you've identified.

For those unfamiliar with the term lookalike modeling, it is the practice of building larger audiences from smaller segments to create greater reach for your marketing. The larger audience reflects the benchmark characteristics of the original audience. In the context of marketing, lookalike modeling can be used to reach new prospects that look like your most loyal and engaged fans. According to a Nielsen study, lookalike modeling can increase results by 2-3x over standard targeting.

The simplest way to figure out who your target audience should be is to figure out who your current audience is, then find more people like that. Fortunately, it doesn't take much to get started down this path.

Number 4:
Rethink Schedule Posters

Schedule posters in their current form are a great and inexpensive way to reward fans. Handing them out to fans at events who take them home to their kids or asking the local bars and restaurants to hang them in the windows is a cheap and easy way to make sure your brand is in front of people on a consistent basis. They can also be valuable as a recruiting tool. Showing incoming student-athletes that they might be featured on a poster if they come to your school is one more drop in the bucket in convincing them to choose you over their other options. However, I could also argue that since every school does schedule posters, this doesn't really give anyone a leg up over anyone else. In this way, it's just become something everyone does because you can't *not* do them.

Unfortunately though, I think that's pretty much the only value schedule posters provide.

That's not to say they don't provide value. They keep coaches happy and they help with recruiting. They reward die-hard fans and keep your brand in front of potential new fans. However, in their current form, schedule posters can hardly be considered a valuable marketing tool in terms of affecting a fan's decision to attend an event.

Additionally, schedule posters have become an arms race where everyone in the nation is competing for who has the best one. But they're not judged on effectiveness to achieve their original mission (driving attendance). They're judged based on whose poster looks the coolest. You're spending thousands of dollars on over-the-top photography and unique printing techniques, plus hours and hours of design time to ensure that your poster makes someone's top 50 list. Why? So you can pat yourselves on the back?

Don't get me wrong. I've made a career off schedule posters. I *love* schedule posters. To be honest, I love it when Old Hat's posters make it onto those top 50 lists. However, I think it's interesting to note that of the top 25 best designed posters on the 2017 Top 50 list (as decided by the most popular resource for such lists on Twitter), only 9 of the teams they were for had increases in attendance from 2016 to 2017. This would indicate that we're falling victim to design for design's sake rather than trying to achieve results with one of the most visible and popular marketing tools we have.

The first thing you need to do when it comes to schedule posters is make a decision on what you want them to be. If you're content with them being something that makes coaches happy, aids in recruiting and/or rewards fans, great. There's nothing wrong with that so keep plugging along making amazing looking posters. However, if you'd like for your posters to actually help drive attendance, you need to start treating them as strategically thought out advertisements, not promotional items.

And how do you do that? By this time, you've decided what you're selling and you've done some data analysis to figure out who and where you should be targeting. Try positioning those schedule posters to target the potential fans you've identified through your research and insight. If you think you should be targeting single men who will be coming to games with their buddies, make sure the poster appeals to that demographic. If you're targeting students, spend a little time making sure the poster highlights the things most appealing to that group.

The most important thing is to pick a group and target them. You can't reach everyone so find a large group you want to target and go for it. That also means abandoning pointless taglines that don't actually mean anything. A simple headline (or tagline) that targets the right people is far better than a super creative tagline that targets no one.

Finally, keep in mind if you go this route, it doesn't mean your posters are going to cease to be good recruiting tools or fun promo items for die-hard fans. Posters *can* be both. But you have to create your strategy first and let the design come second.

Number 5: Answer Questions

There was a time not long ago when fans would go to an organization's website to look for the answers to questions about the sporting event they wanted to attend. Where do I buy tickets? Where can I park? How do I get there? Are there apparel vendors in the arena? And so on. I'm sure that as you're reading this, you have a hundred questions going through your mind that you've answered from fans over the years. Generally, fans asked these questions first in their heads and then went to the website to find the answer. If the website was well organized, they might find the answer but if not, the question went unanswered or the fan had to call the main office to find the answer.

Those days are long gone. Today, fans expect instant gratification. They rarely seek answers by going directly to a website. Instead they just Google it. Did you know that 93% of online experiences now begin with a search engine? And we're already past the days of Googling generic terms like "UNC football game day parking," or "food at Michigan Stadium." People don't type their questions anymore, they speak them. When you ask a question verbally, you get more specific.

Where can I park at UNC football games?

What kind of food do they have at Michigan Stadium?

There are two things to keep in mind here: single source and SEO.

Single Source

Your goal should be to make your website the best single source for answers to the types of questions your fans ask. Get your team together (ticket office, development office, marketing office, etc.) and make a list of questions they get asked by fans on a regular basis. Develop answers to every single one of these questions and post all of that information in a single area of your website.

This may sound fairly pedestrian to some of you. *Seriously? You're suggesting we create an FAQ page?* Yes. I am.

I did a test and Googled questions like those above for

no less than 25 athletics programs. I asked the same list of questions for every program and almost without fail, I was directed to different sources for each answer at every program. The majority of the time, the top sources in the list weren't even affiliated with the program in question and it was rare that any of the sources fully answered my question.

Giving your fans a single source to find answers to every question they might have about buying tickets to and attending your events should be priority #1 for every athletics program. The easiest way to alienate fans and allow them to choose one of your "opponents" over you is to make it difficult to find information about you. Think about the last time you wanted information on a business you were interested in using. For instance, let's say there's a restaurant in town and you think you might want to go there. You get online and find their website. Once you get there, however, their menu is unavailable. They've lost you.

Some sources show that 75% of consumers choose whether or not to use a business based on their experience with its website. If we're not answering the most basic and commonly asked questions by our fans, we're giving them one more reason not to attend.

SEO

Data shows that 47% of people click on one of the first three listings in any online search to find their answer. If you're not in that first three, they're not going to get to you. As I mentioned in my search experiment, it was rare that an athletics program's website came up in the first 3-5 responses on a Google search. Unfortunately, other people are writing more about you than you are and sometimes they're answering your fans' questions incorrectly or incompletely. So how do you get your content to appear higher in Google's search engines?

Google knows that most people search for specific answers at a local level, which is where you operate and where your fans are. Since you are experts in how to answer the most commonly asked questions, it's important that you answer those questions with as much detail as possible. The more details you provide, the more keywords are hit in the search engines and the more people click on your links. The more that happens, the higher you move in the organic search results. Keep in mind that the more questions you answer, the more likely it is that people will be able to find *any* of the answers you provide. If you have budget available, you can also invest in paid search to serve your ads at the top when somebody uses certain key words.

Some athletics programs have created "game day" websites that house a lot of this information. Yet because they haven't gone through the process of answering as many questions as possible and providing detailed answers, these sites are not coming up in Google searches. Simply providing information isn't enough. You have to make sure people can find it.

Action Steps:

1. Get your team together and make a list of the most commonly asked questions (try to get 50, at least).
2. Google those questions and see how quickly you can find answers.
3. Assign someone to answer those questions as clearly and completely as possible.
4. Post those answers on a single page on your primary site or game day site.
5. Start a weekly social media program that highlights one of those most commonly asked questions and provide a link to the answer. This will get traffic to the page and move you up in Google searches.

"As we get customer feedback, we have to make sure we are answering their questions. I believe that without access to information, people make things up. So it's important for us to educate our fan base on what we're doing and why we're doing it. We have to be very transparent. There are so many other things people can be doing with their time, whether it's choosing other forms of entertainment or watching the games from home. Communication, education and transparency are integral to making sure our fans have the information they need so we're not giving them any more reasons to not come to our events."

Markeisha Everett
Assistant Athletic Director for Marketing
University of Pittsburgh

Number 6:
Marketing Automation

Two to three years ago, marketing automation was the shiny new object everyone in the industry was attracted to. Rightfully so, considering how staggering the statistics are around automation and its effectiveness. Research studies show that automation increases sales productivity 14.5% and decreases marketing overhead by more than 12%. Those are actually pretty conservative numbers compared to other studies I've seen.

The struggle has been that when marketing automation arrived on the scene, athletics organizations weren't quite sure what it was or how to use it. As things typically go, big ticketing companies saw the opportunity here and knew they needed to "add this service" to their packages or run the risk of losing out on revenue. So when athletics marketers heard that their contract with their ticket software provider included marketing automation, they took at least a little bit of comfort in that knowledge. Based on the conversations I've had, however, what they're being told is marketing automation is really just a fraction of what the term actually encompasses, so they're not getting the full power or ROI they could be getting.

Every day your fans take actions that can give you key insights into their lives, preferences and buying behaviors. For each visit they take to your website, they're giving you a clue as to what they need and want from you. You can track all of this activity but that doesn't do you much good unless you can do something with the data. That's where marketing automation can and should come in.

Currently, some athletics organizations are using automation to its fullest capacity but most are just scratching the surface, using it for email blasts and tracking link clicks in those emails. Your fans are receiving plenty of messages from you, but most are generic and are being sent to mass lists with little or no audience segmentation. To use automation to its potential, you need to be creating lots of small messages aimed at the different demographics you've identified through your data analytics.

Additionally, now that you have a comprehensive list of commonly asked questions and answers available in one place on your website, your fans will be giving you even greater detail about their needs and wants as long as you have the ability to track them when they get there. On a very base level, if you witness fans seeking information about single game tickets but they do not click to purchase, they should be getting follow-up communication about single game tickets. Automation allows you to get even more in depth to engage your fans on a much more micro level. If they're seeking information on parking, it should trigger an automated email with parking information and a link to purchase a parking pass. Fans searching for concession information should receive offers from your concessionaires or simply receive a list of all the food options in the stadium. Better yet, you might see that they're just kicking the tires to see if they want to purchase tickets. Automation will help you see if they're in your database as having purchased tickets and if not, include that in a follow-up offer.

Make sure to do some A/B testing with your messaging to see what works and what doesn't. Simply sending a message isn't enough. Crafting your messaging to ensure the highest level of engagement is key as well. You can find out if a certain type of email offer is getting more return than others or if one piece of content is more useful to one demographic than another.

There is virtually no limit to the value automation can provide if you have the ability to utilize it to its maximum potential. If you are not currently using marketing automation in any form, start. If you're already using it, call your provider and ask them to tell you exactly what marketing automation is doing for you. See if they can provide you with multiple campaigns and tracking on every page and pixel of your website that you want information from. If you don't like what you hear, look into finding someone that can.

Number 7:
Audit Yourself

There's a saying in the restaurant industry that goes: *Good service can save a bad meal but a good meal can never save bad service.* Personally, I think that's 100% accurate. We

"There are so many factors that go into attendance. From a fan perspective, it's all about the experience. If the food is bad, if the parking is difficult or the ushers are rude, that will keep people from coming back even if the team is undefeated. If you give your fans an amazing experience, from the time they purchase their tickets to when they get in their car to leave the game, it not only makes them want to show up to every game, it makes them want to tell their friends, their family and other alums that it was worth going to the game versus watching from home."

Jamaal Walton
Associate Athletic Director for External Affairs
College of Charleston

know that fans, especially casual and new fans, don't make their decision to attend based on the quality of the product on the field or the opponent. If we adapt the "good service, bad meal" mantra to sporting events, the idea is that an amazing experience can save a bad performance by our team but an amazing performance by the team can't save a terrible experience. I think that's true as well.

No matter how great the team is, a bad experience will drive fans away. If your ticket taker is rude, the food is terrible, the entertainment is boring, the videoboard graphics are bush league, the lines are long, the restrooms are dirty, the amenities are bad, parking is inconvenient or the tailgating is lame, those casual and new fans won't come back.

The only way to truly know the quality of your game day experience is to hire an outside firm to perform a game day audit. This is one area in which doing it yourself just won't work. First of all, your game day responsibilities would make it pretty difficult to go around assessing and scoring each aspect of your game day. But more importantly, auditing your own game day experience would be akin to doing your own work performance review. There's a strong possibility you might be a little biased.

Don't have the budget to bring in an outside firm to conduct a game day audit or want to put together a more quick and dirty audit to get an idea for what's good, bad and ugly about your game day experience? One thing you might consider is pulling together a small group of friends or volunteers to do the audit for you. No, they won't be experts. No, they won't have insight into the inner workings of an athletics game day like a professional firm would. But if you give them a list of questions to answer and areas to rate, along with some basic instructions, you'll at least have *some* feedback to go off of.

Ideally, your group(s) will consist of non-die-hard fans. Die-hards have a tendency to look at everything pertaining to their favorite program with rose-colored glasses so it's unlikely you'll get an unbiased perspective. Plus, you're trying to attract fans that aren't currently coming so you need to seek out people in the casual and new fan categories. For universities, student groups are ideal for this. It should be easy to find students with no previous experience coming to your events. This is one of the most important groups to engage and convert into passionate fans, so their opinions are extremely important. For non-students, seek out local organizations and offer them free tickets in exchange for rating your game day experience. Ask that the participants be people that have never attended or don't normally attend your events.

For the best results, make the audit as simple as possible. Provide a scale for your participants to rate every possible game day element from 1 to 10. Be sure to provide an "n/a" box in case they do not participate in that element. Here is a list of things to rate, just to get you started:

1. Tailgating areas
2. Food vendors (outside stadium)
3. Parking
4. Accessibility
5. Restrooms
6. Concessionaires (service)
7. Ticket takers
8. Overall customer service
9. Amenities
10. Band
11. Cheer
12. Pre-game entertainment
13. In-game entertainment
14. Halftime entertainment
15. Intro/hype video
16. P.A. announcer
17. Promotions

18. Cleanliness
19. In-stadium vendors
20. Food/drink options
21. Audio quality
22. Crowd prompts
23. Connectivity
24. Ushers
25. Stadium exit

There are probably at least 25 more game day elements you have thought of while reading that list. Make a comprehensive list of everything you can think of and rank them by order of importance and choose the top 20-25. Any more than that and your participants will feel like it's a chore and won't give honest, thoughtful feedback. Collect their names and contact information and follow up with anyone that rated anything below a 5. If it's isolated to a couple of people, get suggestions on ways to improve. Then average all the scores for each element. If your overall average is below a 6 for any area, take a very close look at making improvements there. Anything averaging below a 6 might be the one thing that keeps fans from coming back.

Number 8:
Social Media

This section is the longest on the list because there's just so much to tackle when it comes to social media. I could (and probably should) write an entire book on the subject of social media in sports marketing because a small section in this book won't do the topic justice. But I'll hit on some key points to consider.

Platforms

Here are some quick facts about the three most popular social media platforms out there: Facebook, Instagram and Twitter. I'm only focusing on these three because 1) their user base is far greater than any others and 2) these are the three most often used in athletics marketing. LinkedIn and Pinterest have comparative numbers to Twitter, but these platforms are typically not being utilized for sports marketing and in my opinion, aren't the right places to be spending our time. As popular as Snapchat is, only 13% of professional social marketers are using it because it has the lowest percentage of consumer usage out of all the channels.

Facebook
According to Sprout Social, 79% of internet users are still regularly logging into Facebook. Considering that 80% of US adults have access to the Internet, that means Facebook has a massive user base. Nearly 90% of 18-29 year olds use Facebook but it's also the most popular platform for every other age range as well: 84% of 30-49 year olds, 72% of 50-64 year olds and 62% of 65+ year olds use Facebook. As far as gender goes, Facebook skews toward women with 83% of adult women using it compared to 75% of men. Another notable stat: whether you're living in an urban, rural or suburban area, 77% or more of everyone around you is using

Facebook. It's also popular among 75% or more of every income demographic.

Instagram
Instagram, on the other hand, has much lower usage numbers for anyone over 30. About 33% of people ages 30 and older use Instagram, with just 8% among the 65+ group. But 59% of 18-29 year olds use Instagram. This platform skews higher for urban dwellers at 39% compared to around 30% for rural and suburban areas. About the same percentage of people making less than $30,000 per year and above $75,000 per year use Instagram, with the pack in the middle having lower numbers. Meaning, the most and least wealthy people use this platform but the mid-range use it a bit less.

Twitter
Twitter's percentages follow a similar pattern to Instagram's, though Twitter posts overall lower percentages across the board for all demographics. On the high side, 36% of 18-29 year olds use Twitter and on the low end, 10% of the 65+ crowd is tweeting. The big differentiator with Twitter is that it's the only platform where a higher level of education and a higher income indicates a higher likelihood of use. The most educated and most wealthy internet users use Twitter the most. But it's still less than Instagram or Facebook.

Why is this information important? By and large, athletics organizations aren't taking this demographic information into consideration when communicating on social media.

Too often, we are communicating with our fans in the same way (or the wrong way) on our channels despite the fact that the fans following us on each channel are completely different. We also sometimes make the mistake of thinking we have to be on every channel which can cause our message to get diluted because we don't have the time to communicate effectively on all three. We may have the resources to give it 100% on one channel but we end up only being 33% effective because we spread ourselves thin trying to do it all.

Decide where you should be giving it your all and focus there. When you get that perfected, take on the other channels.

Audience Personas

Taking it a step further, consider engaging someone to help create audience personas for each of your social media channels. You know that most Instagram users are in a certain demographic. But you don't know for sure if most of *your* Instagram followers are in that demographic. Research your followers on each platform and create a character/personality that represents the most common user on that channel. If the largest group of Facebook followers is in that 30-49 age group, start there. Then look at the average or median age from that group and the gender breakdown. Give your character as many specific details as possible so you can more effectively understand how to communicate with him/her.

Here's an example of what that could look like:

Facebook
Name: Holli
Age: 38
Profession: Elementary School Teacher
Description: She spends the weekends with her family and loves attending events at her alma mater, East Popcorn State University. She checks Facebook to see what her friends and family are up to and likes to post photos of her children. She is always on the move so she consumes digital data at a quick rate.
Characteristics: Community-oriented, well-liked, clever, social, not detail-oriented
Something she might say: I love tailgating with friends and taking my family to football games but it's so expensive that we usually only go to 1-2 games per year.

Instagram
Name: Phoebe
Age: 28
Profession: Graphic Designer
Description: She pours her heart into her day job and stays up late either binge-watching Netflix or going out with friends. She consumes digital media in her downtime like lunch or over a cup of coffee. She likes good-looking digital media and scrolls right past anything with no creativity behind it.
Characteristics: Fun, driven, sharp, scattered, imaginative, resourceful

<u>Something she might say</u>: I love my alma mater through and through and can't wait to tailgate with my friends this weekend. If one of them has an extra ticket, you can bet I'll be in the stadium!

Twitter
<u>Name</u>: Dan
<u>Age</u>: 45
<u>Profession</u>: Attorney
<u>Description</u>: Attended East Popcorn State for undergrad and law school and has been a fan of EPSU athletics since he was young. He is married with children, coaches little league and plays golf as often as possible. He watches ESPN every morning and every night and he hasn't missed a home football game since his second child was born. He consumes digital media for words and facts.
<u>Characteristics</u>: Hard-working, engaging, funny, stubborn, active
<u>Something he might say</u>: If I make partner this year, I'm going to upgrade to club level seats.

As you can see, just reading those descriptions makes it more clear how you should communicate with those individuals. We can't be all things to all people on our social media channels. Figure out what characteristics represent your largest group of followers on each platform and target them.

Content

There are four stages in the fan journey when deciding whether or not to make a ticket purchase: awareness, consideration, decision and loyalty (or repurchase). Social channels are a great place for content that not only increases awareness but also supports fans through the consideration stage of their decision process. However, 80% or more of athletics marketers concentrate solely on awareness content and ignore the consideration stage in their social media efforts.

"We're on all the major social media platforms and our digital team does an amazing job customizing content on all of them. But something we're really proud of is the way we utilize Twitter. We have an account for our mascot, Brutus, and our main Ohio State Athletics account. We leverage our mascot account to be more of a fun, light-hearted engagement tool. This affords us an opportunity to really have a conversation with our fans. Whereas our main athletics account is more for pushing out information to our fans. Having those two different accounts allows our digital team to toggle between the two and gives us more opportunities to engage with our fans."

Tyler Jones
Assistant Athletics Director for Fan Engagement
The Ohio State University

What does consideration stage content look like? The consideration stage is when fans are trying to determine if they're going to choose attending the game over other opportunities. They are considering whether to attend the game in person, watch it on TV (either at home or another venue), or ignore the event altogether and go to the lake. It's in this stage where we should be providing ticket purchasing offers and calls to action, sharing videos about why our option for entertainment is better than our competition and highlighting the reasons being *at* the event is the right choice.

In the "emotional vs. rational" argument, awareness content is the emotionally *exciting* content that gets people pumped about our programs. But if it's not followed up with the rational consideration content, we're losing potential fans.

What Fans Want

The number one type of content consumers want from brands on social is links to more information, followed by photos/images, behind-the-scenes video, text/conversations and finally, produced/edited photos. What does this mean for athletics organizations? It means we should be giving our fans something real. They like seeing photos but only if they're candid, unstaged images. They want to see our athletes in a behind-the-scenes way. What do they care least about seeing on social media? Videos and images we've spent hours producing with high-impact visuals and motion graphics. We also need to be giving them something to click on. Simply putting visuals out there does little to nudge your fans into taking action.

A friend in the industry told me about a time when someone on his video team spent 11 hours producing a hype video for their tennis team. The video was really, really good. But on social media, it got less than 20 views. Think about that: 11 hours of work for 20 views. Fans want something real, not produced. Save the hype videos for the videoboard.

The top three content priorities for fans are posts about sales/discounts, posts that showcase new products and services, and posts that teach something. We may not have sales and discounts but we probably do have plenty to say about special offers (i.e. mini-packs, single game tickets, etc.). While we probably don't have much in the way of new products either, we can definitely teach with our content and share new information about our players, our program or our venues.

What we should be doing instead of spending 11 hours producing impressive content, is spend that time producing useful content. Think back to that list you made of all the questions your fans ask you. Now think about how many times you've watched *Tasty* videos on Facebook showing you the step-by-step process for making a potato casserole (with spiral cut potatoes) you will *never* make. Consumers love content like that. How can that translate to your list of questions? Can you shoot how-to videos to answer some of the most commonly asked questions? The opportunities are there, you just have to look for them.

Quick Tips

1) Nearly half of all social media users have reached out to a brand for customer service issues. Monitor your channels and if a fan asks a question, ensure they get a response.

2) Influencer marketing has become a very effective and popular tool for increasing engagement. However, research shows that 61% of people say they are more likely to consider a purchase if it's recommended by a friend vs. only 36% if it's a well-known influencer or celebrity. Consider using the less expensive and more effective option of friend and employee advocacy in place of influencer marketing.

3) Don't worry about ROI on social media. Only 14% of social marketers say they're able to quantify revenue from social. Focus on brand awareness and consideration marketing.

4) When it comes to engagement and sharing, keep in mind that the top three types of posts that get both the most engagement and the most shares are: posts that entertain, posts that inspire and posts about special offers. If your goal is to engage fans and get them to share your posts, concentrate on creating this type of content.

5) If you can't highlight the quality wins of your teams, try highlighting the quality of character of your programs' coaches and players. In the 2016 fan survey referenced earlier in this book, we asked fans if they are more likely to support a team if they believe the coaches and/or athletes are of good character. As you'd imagine, the vast majority of people said they would. Almost 90% of people stated that they would either "probably" or "definitely" be more likely to support a team if they felt the coaches and/or athletes were of good character. More than half (56%) of respondents said that the quality of a team's coaches and/or athletes influenced their own feelings toward that team either "most of the time" or "always." The rest fell into the "sometimes" category while less than 1% of people stated that character "never" influences their feelings toward a team.

Number 9:
Engaging the Squirrel Generation

According to *Fast Company,* Gen Z will make up 40% of all consumers by 2020. Considering that this generation consists of those born after 1995, all of your students are a part of this generation. Like every generation before them, they're different than their predecessors. Therefore marketing to them is, by default, different than marketing to previous generations. The problem is that as fast as our world is changing now, what drives consumer behavior from generation to generation changes much more quickly than in the past.

We all know that today's students are tomorrow's season ticket holders. How can we build loyalty now with a generation that is as easily distracted as "Dug" from the movie *UP*? *Squirrel!*

Retire the Sandwich Boards

I probably walk across no less than 30 college campuses every year and on virtually every one of them, I see sandwich boards advertising athletics events coming up that day or evening. Unfortunately, I'm probably the only person on campus who's seeing them because I'm the only one intentionally looking at my surroundings.

Gen Z lives on their devices. Chances are they're going to walk by that sandwich board a few times a day and never once notice that it's there because they're staring at their smartphone. That means you've wasted the time of your graphic designer and wasted your interns' time by asking them to go put the sandwich boards up. Invest that time more wisely by meeting your students where they live – on their devices.

Highlight a Cause

Gen Z doesn't want to be sold. They've grown up in a world that allows them to research sales claims in seconds and they see through sales tactics very easily. They do, however, like to be a part of a cause. They like to support values and social good. Fortunately, athletics organizations have a wealth of opportunities to highlight the social good they provide, especially at the collegiate level (see my first book, *If Not for Athletics*). Athletics does so much good for humanity. Highlight that in your marketing to Gen Z and you'll see greater engagement.

> "We put out a lot of edgy, high-impact, flashy 6-second videos on our social media platforms targeted at Gen Z. We've done the research and we know that we have 7 seconds to grab their attention. So you'll see a lot of 6-second videos on the channels where they follow us. Baby Boomers want long form features. They want to sit down and watch it. But Gen Z wants content they can view while they're walking from one class to the next. So we create that content and tag it with when the next game is. Or we show them a product we're going to have at our next game. Some recent research has shown that today's students want a cool product over an experience. Branded games, pop sockets... whatever it is, Gen Z wants it and they want it quickly. So we create short, snackable content for the channels Gen Z follows us on and custom content for the older generations for the channels they're most likely to follow us on."
>
> Leah Beasley
> *Executive Senior Associate Athletics Director for External Affairs*
> Mississippi State University

Sell the Experience

With Gen Z, the product you're selling is the experience, not the event. Focus on what the experience is going to do for them and how they will benefit from it. They know what's going to be happening on the field so only use the event as the stage for something greater. Market to Gen Z by telling them what will be the result of them attending. Tune into what gets them excited and engaged. Take advantage of the fact that this generation cares less about what's happening on the field/court than any before them.

Peer Experiences

Unlike most generations before them, Gen Z is unaffected by celebrity endorsement. They are far more influenced by their peers and "real" people they follow on YouTube. They're less interested in what some millionaire tells them they should own or do, and more interested in what others like them are owning or doing. Good news: you have thousands of students on campus you can use to tell your story for you. We've all heard and read about the importance of "influencer marketing" in connecting with Gen Z. While you may not have the resources to hire the most followed influencers to promote your athletics events, you do have thousands of potential influencers right in front of you. Give student fans a great experience and encourage them to share that experience with others.

Social Natives

Unlike those of us who remember when a desktop computer was a luxury item and email was new technology, Gen Z sees both of these as necessary evils. They don't surf the web on their computer unless they're doing research for a paper they're writing; they mostly use email for contacting professors and applying for jobs. Forget sending them email marketing. Instead, focus on native apps and social media. Optimize your content to be relevant to the way Gen Z prefers to consume it: on their phone. If you have the means, this is the one group I'd recommend connecting with via Snapchat. However, if you can't do Snapchat well you may end up shooting yourself in the foot. Gen Z will see through poor execution on any social media platform, especially Snapchat. If you have smart interns you can trust, ask them for help getting it right. Otherwise, stick with Instagram.

Make It Move

Don't waste your time with photos or still graphics when

> "You only have a few seconds to get their attention. They are being bombarded with so many different messages every day. We have to be interesting enough, creative enough and entertaining enough to break through all of that."
>
> Brian Bowsher
> *Chief Marketing Officer*
> University of Washington

marketing to Gen Z. They are accustomed to being entertained so even if it's a graphic advertising an upcoming event, make it move. Gen Z, unlike their Millennial predecessors, doesn't mind being advertised to. But your content has to be entertaining and it needs to be short. While Millennials have an alarmingly short attention span of 12 seconds, Gen Z will only last 7-8 seconds. We have to hook them and we have to do it fast. So if you're advertising events and trying to get them to click on something, keep it brief. Once you win their attention in those first 7-8 seconds, Gen Z is likely to stick around for 1-3 minutes. That means you need to plan both short-form and medium-form content that's engaging and entertaining.

Keep It Real

Gen Z doesn't mind being advertised to, as long as you're calling a spade a spade. What they do mind is marketing or advertising that's disingenuous. Authenticity matters to this crowd. If it looks phony, they're not interested. For example, American Eagle had great success when they implemented a "no-photoshop" policy in their advertising in 2014. Think about how that principle can apply to your own marketing. Make sure what you're putting out there is genuine and unscripted.

Scrap the Loyalty Programs

Another difference between Millennials and Gen Z is their desire to be a part of loyalty programs. While nearly half of Millennials find value in loyalty programs, that percentage drops to 30% for the next generation. Gen Z wants to make decisions on their own terms, not because they've been roped into some program that rewards their repeat purchases. Loyalty programs are expensive and time consuming. With the students you have on campus right now, this type of effort won't produce the ROI you're looking for.

Number 10:
Onboarding

On average, a *loyal* customer is worth about ten times the value of their original purchase. A loyal *fan* on the other hand, could be worth an exponentially higher amount due to the emotional attachment fans form for their favorite sports teams over years and decades. The key is turning those casual and new fans into loyal, die-hard fans, which is no easy task. One highly effective way to gain fan loyalty is by giving them an amazing customer service experience.

Statistics abound highlighting the loyalty that is created when brands do a great job at customer service. A few of them:

- 55% of people say they will pay more for good customer service.
- 70% of customers' satisfaction is based on how they feel they are being treated.

> "We are very aware that we are asking fans to leave their homes with their giant TVs and refrigerator full of pop to come spend the weekend with us. What are we doing to make sure we are giving them an experience that makes them want to keep coming back? It comes down to a consistency in customer service."
>
> **Drew Martin**
> *Executive Senior Associate Athletics Director for External Affairs*
> University of Texas

- 73% of people state they love certain brands because of the customer service they receive.
- 89% of consumers have stopped doing business with a brand due to poor customer service.

We can no longer subscribe to the idea that the moment we sell a ticket to a potential fan is the moment we win them over. Loyalty does not begin until we've achieved our first success with that fan. This means that your fans' first experience with you is absolutely critical. It's not enough to simply sell them a ticket through a streamlined online process or trained sales rep. The buying experience does not end there. Fans must be onboarded properly as well in order to begin the conversion from casual/new fan to die-hard.

What is onboarding? It's the journey you take your fans on to get them from purchasing a ticket to walking in the gates of your facility. Unfortunately, an extremely high percentage of athletics organizations I spoke with told me that they aren't managing this journey in any way. This might be a big reason why we see attendance dropping.

What does onboarding look like in athletics? Any number of things, and it may vary from organization to organization. Here are a few steps you can take to begin developing your own comprehensive onboarding process.

1) Determine if you have an onboarding process at all. Do you communicate with a ticket purchaser after the purchase is made or do you just sell the ticket and hope they show up?

2) If you don't have an onboarding process, start small. Go back to that list of frequently asked questions you made and figure out which ones pertain to new ticket purchasers. Then develop a series of email blasts that get sent out to those fans leading up to the game. Don't try to answer all questions in one fell swoop. Space them out so as not to overwhelm your fans.

3) If you do have an onboarding process, look for ways to improve it. Are you just answering questions or are you giving them the "wow" factor that makes them feel like you really care? Remember that more than half of your fans will pay more if they feel like they're receiving above average customer service. And if they have a bad experience, nearly all of them may consider leaving you.

4) If your organization is highly advanced and has a robust marketing automation platform, develop a customized email onboarding system that makes your fans feel unique. Show them that you know who they are specifically and communicate to them directly. If they purchase seats in section 152, make sure they know what concessions are available in that section and the nearest location for other menu items. Highlight the nearest parking areas closest to the gates where they should enter for easiest access to their seats. There are a hundred ways you can make your fans feel like you know who they are. Find them.

Your fans are emotionally invested in your athletics program. Show them that you are invested in them and you'll see a much greater loyalty and return on investment.

Number 11:
Project Costs

I received a call about a year ago from a mid-major athletics department that was about to launch a $70 million capital campaign and wanted to get an estimate on a website to help with fundraising and marketing for the campaign. I told them that we'd done sites like these for as much as $250,000 and for as little as $25,000. What they were describing was on the lower end of that spectrum so I was confident that we could do something for around the $25k figure. He had a bit of sticker shock and told me that their max budget for the project was about $7,500.

A website can be an amazing tool for generating interest, support and donations for a capital campaign. In fact, the websites we've developed have assisted in raising more than a billion dollars for various capital campaigns. But this isn't an advertisement for Old Hat's web services. It's an argument for the proper investment into marketing tools, regardless of who you contract to produce them.

The university I referenced above wasn't even willing to spend 1% of the campaign funds on the one tool that would have done them the most good in helping them raise those funds. That's understandable, of course. One percent would have been $700,000 which is a lot to pay for a website. I do think .01% is reasonable though. That would equate to $70,000 which would have actually been more than enough to produce a pretty amazing website, plus a marketing automation campaign, a social media strategy and still have some left over for a digital media campaign. This would have undoubtedly helped them reach their goal more quickly but instead, they only wanted to spend 0.001% of their capital campaign on what could have been the campaign's most effective marketing and fundraising tool.

Here's another example. A good friend told me of a time he was approached by Google about a $2,000 digital ad spend that they expected to see a 6x return on but they *guaranteed* would result in at least a 3x return. He went to his superior to ask for the authorization to spend the money and was met with, "Do you have $2,000 in your budget?" He responded by saying that no, he did not, because this was not anticipated and he did not budget for it. He was not permitted to spend the $2k.

I have heard so many stories just like that when talking to athletics marketers and fundraisers. People in this industry are either unwilling or unable to properly invest in marketing. I believe this is the number one problem preventing athletics organizations from being effective with their marketing tactics. I have been in business for 15 years and have found that there might not be any cliché that rings more true than this one: *you must spend money to make money.* But the athletics industry seems to operate under the exact opposite philosophy. While "a penny saved is a penny earned" may be true, sticking to that idea won't help you get results with your marketing or fundraising.

Proper marketing and advertising in virtually any industry can result in a 10% growth in revenue. For athletics, if you're currently putting 50,000 people in your stadium at $50 per fan, a 10% increase would mean $250,000 per game, or $1.5 million over the course of a typical football season. Yet for some reason, asking an athletics department to spend $150,000 (10% of the proposed increase) on the marketing that would be necessary to achieve this growth is met with complete shock.

I can assure you that if you approached any corporation in

the world (including mine) and told them that you could increase their revenue by 10% in exchange for 10% of that revenue, they'd jump at it. Every time. In athletics, however, we want to spend 0.001% on one of the most vital tools for our marketing efforts and then are surprised when it doesn't produce the desired results.

We must start looking at marketing costs as project costs. The cost of building a new facility includes architecture, engineering, land purchase, construction and much more. Marketing should be included in that, especially if you're trying to raise funds to pay for it. The same goes for ticket sales. If you want to produce more revenue, marketing costs should, at a minimum, be 10% of what you're hoping to produce *in excess* of what you're expecting in automatic renewals.

Number 12:
Learn Your Per Caps

In chapter 9, I talked about utilizing a portion of the revenue from your concession and apparel vendors to help pay for strategic marketing initiatives. But to do that, you have to know your "per caps," or the amount of money each fan spends after ticket cost once they enter your stadium or arena.

If your organization has this information available, read it and memorize it. Do the math on how much additional revenue you can produce for your organization for each additional fan that attends your events. You never know when this knowledge can come in handy.

If your organization doesn't have this information, do some digging and develop a report that outlines it all. Then share it with your colleagues. They'll be better for it and you'll look like a hero.

Sports programs are an economic boon for your communities and universities. From local retailers to bars/ restaurants to people selling parking in their front yard, everyone is making money off of you. Sometimes you get a cut of those dollars and other times you don't. If you are getting a cut, you have to know what that cut is. Everyone working in an athletics organization in any external role should be able to rattle off the concession and apparel per caps for every ticketed sport they sponsor. Then keep that knowledge in your back pocket and use it when the opportunity arises.

Number 13:
Crazy Ideas

Since the dawn of time, all of the greatest ideas once seemed crazy. The idea that we'd be able to carry around tiny computers in our hands and communicate with the entire world by tapping a touchscreen was once just a crazy idea. Now every one of us has one in our pocket. Even the idea that we'd be able to flip a switch and illuminate a room using a little glass bulb with copper wires in it seemed crazy once upon a time. Now it sounds crazy to think there was a time we *couldn't* do that.

From a sports marketing perspective, the concept of reducing concession prices at Mercedes-Benz Stadium in Atlanta sounded crazy at first. It went against the year-over-year trend of increasing prices at stadium concession stands. However, somebody at the top realized that these increases seemed to be driving fans away. So the ownership group of the Atlanta Falcons introduced "Fan First Menu Pricing" which effectively reduced the price of food and beverage in the stadium by 50 percent. This resulted in fans showing up early, taking greater advantage of more affordable concessions, and having a better game day experience in the process. It also resulted in a 16% increase in food and beverage revenue versus the previous year in their old stadium. The lower prices are also thought to have contributed to additional spending on apparel as revenue increased 88% in that category.

When this crazy idea was announced, the industry's response was to ignore it, assuming money was going to be left on the table. Now that the idea doesn't seem so crazy after all, multiple other professional and college sports programs are following suit.

Great leaders and great organizations encourage crazy ideas. When you're fighting to keep your current fans and bring in new fans, you need crazy ideas to do it. Create an environment in your organization that encourages your staff to develop and recommend crazy ideas. Go a step further and require that everyone comes up with at least one crazy idea each quarter. Not all of those ideas can or should be implemented. Not all that get implemented will work. But failure is okay, as long as you're trying. At some point, you just might hit on an idea that the rest of the industry ignores at first and then scrambles to replicate.

"The traditions that all of us in collegiate athletics are fortunate enough to be stewards of were, at one point, just crazy ideas. They were something someone thought of attempting and gave it a shot. It may have been organic or it may have been forced but at one point it wasn't a tradition, it was just an idea."

Brad Wurthman
Senior Associate Athletics Director for External Operations
Virginia Tech

POSTGAME

From the time I sent the manuscript of this book to my editor to the time it came back with edits, at least 19 articles came out about declining attendance in college football. That's a staggering number and those are just the articles I *saw*. There have to have been at least 19 more that I didn't come across.

The problem isn't only with college football, or even college sports in general. In addition to those 19, I read articles about declining attendance in both Major and Minor League Baseball, NFL, NBA, the Canadian Football League and even UFC and WWE. Leagues and front offices all over the country are scrambling to figure out ways to bring fans back to their stadiums and arenas. Many are trying the fan-friendly concession pricing trend and a wide array of other tactics to appeal to fans but unfortunately, I saw a handful of comments from owners and marketers along the lines of, *We need to start by winning games.* Imagine if Ford's marketing department said, *Our F-150 really isn't very good this year. Once they start making better trucks, people will start buying them.*

We can't sit around waiting for our product to get better before we figure out a way to market it.

In order for one team to win, another team has to lose. By the nature of sports, some teams are going to have losing seasons no matter what. We can't all be winning. Which means that unless we're fortunate enough to work somewhere that hardly ever loses, we have to figure out a way to draw fans in regardless of how good our teams are. We know it's possible because plenty of teams are doing it. What I hope this book has done is provide you with a new way of looking at sports marketing that will allow you to be more strategic with your overall marketing plans *and* provide you with some action steps you can take immediately to start making improvements to your approach.

No matter what league we work in or what sport we're charged with building engagement for, we all need a strategy for driving attendance. And winning is *not* a strategy.

Thank You

This book is the culmination of three years worth of research and the contributions of countless individuals. I cannot begin to list them all but I must call out a few that have most directly impacted my ability to write it.

My wife, Holli, who was the one that convinced me not to try to combine this book with my previous. That decision made both books better by leaps and bounds. Her patience and encouragement (and copy-editing) truly made this book possible.

Megan E. Miranda who not only edited the book but also helped conduct much of the research upon which it is based.

The entire staff at Old Hat who strongly encouraged me to write this book and were patient with me throughout the process.

David Chapin whose guidance led to my first "fan journey" diagram which served as the basis for much of this book.

To everyone who allowed me to use their quotes throughout.

Brad Wurthman, a great friend with whom I have shared countless conversations about the ideas expressed in this book and the person I first heard use the phrase, "winning is not a strategy."

Zac Logsdon

Zac has written two books on athletics and is a frequent speaker around the country on sports marketing, fan behavior and the positive impact of sports.

@zaclogsdon
www.zaclogsdon.com
www.ifnotforathletics.com

Zac is also CEO and Founder of Old Hat, a strategic marketing agency founded in 2004 that has worked with more than 150 sports organizations to help them drive attendance, enhance the game experience for fans and improve fundraising efforts.

www.oldhatcreative.com

Bulk quantities of *Winning is Not a Strategy* are available for purchase at a reduced rate for sports organizations and sports administration educational programs. To purchase, visit the link below:

www.winningisnotastrategy.com